World Economic and Financial Surveys

Selected Topic
Expanded and updated from the IMF's
Global Financial Stability Report

Emerging Local Securities and Derivatives Markets

Donald J. Mathieson
Jorge E. Roldos
Ramana Ramaswamy
Anna Ilyina

International Monetary Fund
2004

© 2004 International Monetary Fund

Production: IMF Multimedia Services Division
Cover: Phil Torsani
Photo: Padraic Hughes
Figures: Theodore F. Peters, Jr.

ISBN 1-58906-291-4
ISSN 0258-7440

Price: US$49.00
(US$46.00 to full-time faculty members and
students at universities and colleges)

Please send orders to:
International Monetary Fund, Publication Services
700 19th Street, N.W., Washington, D.C. 20431, U.S.A.
Tel.: (202) 623-7430   Telefax: (202) 623-7201
E-mail: publications@imf.org
Internet: http://www.imf.org

recycled paper

CONTENTS

Preface	v
Chapter I. Local Securities and Derivatives Markets in Emerging Markets: Selected Policy Issues	**1**
Donald J. Mathieson and Jorge E. Roldos	
Local Markets as Self-Insurance Against Volatile Capital Flows	2
Extent of Securities Market Development as an Alternative Source of Funding	5
Common Practices in Emerging Local Securities Markets	10
Selected Policy Issues	13
Conclusion	23
Chapter II. Emerging Local Bond Markets	**24**
Jorge E. Roldos	
Size and Structure of Global Bond Markets	24
Local Bond Markets as an Alternative Source of Funding	25
Secondary Markets and the Role of Foreign Investors	41
Conclusion	45
Chapter III. Emerging Equity Markets	**46**
Ramana Ramaswamy	
Emerging Market Equities as an Asset Class for Foreign Investors	46
Domestic Equity as an Alternative Source of Funding	54
Conclusions	65
Chapter IV. The Role of Financial Derivatives in Emerging Markets	**69**
Anna Ilyina	
Overview of Derivatives Markets in Emerging Economies	69
Local Derivatives Markets and Capital Flows to Emerging Economies	83
The Role of Derivatives in Emerging Market Crises	87
Concluding Remarks	90
Bibliography	**91**

Boxes

1. An International Solution for the Original Sin	16
2. Indexed Bonds	30
3. External Refinancing Risk in Latin America	36
4. Local Corporate Bond Market in Russia	38
5. The Equity Market in Russia	61
6. The Equity Market in China	66

7. The Bolsa de Mercadorias & Futuros of São Paulo ... 73
8. Credit Default Swap Spreads in Emerging Markets ... 82

Tables

1. Reserves: Level and Ratio to GDP ... 3
2. Private Sector ... 6
3. Public Sector ... 8
4. Total of All Sectors ... 9
5. Size and Structure of the Global Bond Market in 2002 ... 25
6. Selected Emerging Local Bond Markets: Amounts Outstanding ... 27
7. Emerging Market Debt Trading Volume Survey ... 42
8. Equity and Bond Returns ... 48
9. Notional Amounts Outstanding of the Over-The-Counter and Exchange-Traded Derivatives ... 70
10. Average Daily Turnover in the Over-The-Counter Derivatives Markets ... 71
11. Exchange-Traded Options and Futures Contract Trading Volume, 2002 ... 75

Figures

1. Chile: Amount Outstanding of Private Nonfinancial Sector Bonds ... 14
2. Corporate Bond Issuance in Selected Emerging Markets ... 34
3. Selected Countries Domestic Yield Curves ... 44
4. Equity and Bond Performances ... 48
5. Risk-Return Trade-Off for Combinations of Emerging Market Stocks and U.S. Stocks ... 50
6. Valuation Indicators in Emerging Equity Markets ... 51
7. Correlations Between Returns in Emerging and U.S. Equity Markets ... 52
8. Stock Market Capitalization and Bank Credit ... 55
9. Domestic and International Equity Issuance ... 55
10. International Equity Issuance by IPO and Privatization: Numbers ... 56
11. International Equity Issuance by IPO and Privatization: Billions of Dollars ... 57
12. Monthly Dollar Trading Volume for Selected Asian Countries ... 58
13. Monthly Dollar Trading Volume for Selected Latin American Countries ... 59
14. Monthly Dollar Trading Volume for Selected European Countries ... 60
15. Average Daily Turnover in the South African Foreign-Exchange Market by Type of Transaction ... 72
16. Average Daily Turnover in the South African Foreign-Exchange Swap Market ... 72
17. Mexican Bond Issuance and Interest Rate Futures ... 76
18. Korean Government Bond Futures ... 78
19. Average Daily Trading Volumes in Equity Index Derivatives in Asia ... 79
20. KOSPI 200 Index Futures: Cumulative Net Purchases ... 79
21. International Bond and Loan Issuance and Derivatives Trading Volume in Brazil ... 85

PREFACE

Much of the recent interest in developing local securities and derivatives markets stems from the experience of many emerging markets with volatile international capital flows and financial crises during the 1990s. Indeed, "sudden stops" (or even reversals) of capital flows were often key features of many of the most severe balance of payments and systemic banking crises of the period (particularly in the Mexican crisis of 1995 and the Asian crisis of 1997). The banking system problems in turn reflected the debt-servicing difficulties of the domestic corporates, especially those with large foreign currency debts. More generally, the volatility of capital flows since the mid-1990s has raised two issues: how emerging markets can achieve more stable access to international capital markets and how these economies can cope with whatever volatility does occur. While establishing sound and sustainable macroeconomic policies has been one obvious element in strengthening domestic economic fundamentals and perceived creditworthiness, many emerging markets have taken additional measures designed to "self-insure" against volatile capital flows. These measures have included:

- changes in external asset and liability management practices;
- adapting exchange rate arrangements to the degree of capital account openness;
- strengthening domestic financial institutions and enhancing prudential supervision and regulation to increase resilience to volatility; and
- developing local securities and derivatives markets to provide an alternative source of funding for the public and corporate sectors and to facilitate the management of the financial risks associated with periods of high asset price volatility.

This report examines two key aspects of this self-insurance policy, namely the extent to which emerging markets have developed local securities and derivatives and what key policy issues have arisen as a result. The information used in this report was gathered through a series of missions to international financial centers and to selected emerging markets between February and May 2002. The discussions took place in Brazil, Chile, China, Hong Kong SAR, Hungary, Poland, Russia, Singapore, Thailand, the United Kingdom, and the United States. The report was directed by Donald J. Mathieson, Chief of the IMF's Emerging Markets Surveillance Division, and Jorge Roldos, Deputy Chief of the same division. Contributors to the study from the IMF's International Capital Markets Department included Torbjorn Becker, Jorge Chan-Lau, Anna Ilyina, Ramana Ramaswamy, Manmohan Singh, R. Todd Smith, and Amadou Sy. In addition, Ivan Guerra, Silvia Iorgova, Anne Jansen, and Peter Tran provided research assistance. Elsa Portaro, Ramanjeet Singh, and Joan Wise provided expert word processing assistance. Jeff Hayden of the External Relations Department edited the manuscript and coordinated production of the report.

CHAPTER I: LOCAL SECURITIES AND DERIVATIVES MARKETS IN EMERGING MARKETS: SELECTED POLICY ISSUES

Donald J. Mathieson and Jorge E. Roldos

The development of local securities and derivatives markets is just one response of many emerging markets to global volatility since the mid-1990s, particularly the sudden losses of access to international capital markets and periods of high global asset price volatility. This chapter analyzes key policy issues related to the role of these markets as an alternative source of funding for sovereign and corporate entities and a means of attracting foreign capital inflows. Subsequent chapters examine the development of local bond, equity, and derivatives markets in emerging markets.

The capital flow and asset price volatility that has characterized the global financial system since the mid-1990s has raised the issue of how emerging markets' economic and financial systems can be made more resilient to such volatility. Clearly, the loss of access to international markets associated with unsustainable macroeconomic and exchange rate policies can be best addressed by adopting stronger domestic policies. However, coping with a loss of market access associated with contagion from a crisis in other emerging markets and/or volatility in capital flows and asset prices associated with developments in mature markets is a more complex issue. Many emerging markets have adopted a variety of measures to self-insure against such volatility. While these measures have differed across regions, they typically have included changing sovereign external asset and liability management practices; adapting exchange rate arrangements to the degree of capital account openness; strengthening domestic financial institutions and enhancing prudential supervision and regulation in order to increase resilience to volatility; and developing local securities and derivatives markets.

The development of local securities and derivatives markets is seen as a means of creating a more stable source of local currency funding for both the public and corporate sectors, thereby mitigating the funding difficulties created by "sudden stops" in cross-border capital flows and reducing dependence on bank credit as a source of funding. In addition, the development of these markets is seen as a vehicle for improving the efficiency and stability of financial intermediation, reducing the currency and maturity mismatches associated with cross-border lending, and creating new opportunities and instruments for hedging various financial and exchange rate risks.

The measures adopted to further the development of local securities and derivatives markets have typically encompassed efforts to strengthen market infrastructure and create benchmark issues, expand the set of institutional investors, and improve corporate governance and transparency. However, there are several key policy areas where no consensus has emerged regarding either the factors that will influence the likely outcomes or the most appropriate policies. Issues remain regarding:
- the use of instruments indexed to changes in such variables as the price level and exchange rates;
- the government's role in promoting the development of local equity markets;
- the role of foreign investors in local securities and derivatives markets;
- the degree of development of local derivatives markets; and
- the sequencing of reforms in local securities and derivatives markets.

This chapter first examines how the recent interest in local securities and derivatives markets is part of a response to international capital flow and asset price volatility and to systemic banking crises. It then reviews the extent to which local securities markets have become an important source of funding for the corporate and public sectors, and considers the most common measures used to develop local securities and derivatives markets. The chapter concludes with a discussion of "gray areas" concerning policies related to developing these markets.

Local Markets as Self-Insurance Against Volatile Capital Flows

Much of the recent interest in developing local securities and derivatives markets reflects the experience of many emerging markets with international capital flows, unstable asset prices, and systemic banking crises. While the scale of gross and net private capital flows rose steadily during the first half of the 1990s, the remainder of the 1990s witnessed greater volatility of capital flows, as well as a decline in the overall level of flows (especially after 1997).[1] Moreover, "sudden stops" (or even reversals) of capital flows were often key features of many of the most severe balance of payments and systemic banking crises of the period (particularly in the Mexican crisis of 1995 and the Asian crisis of 1997).[2] To an important degree, the banking system problems in turn reflected the debt-servicing difficulties of domestic corporates, especially those with large foreign currency debt.

While sudden stops in capital flows often reflected increased investor concerns about weaknesses in domestic economic and political fundamentals and domestic financial systems in emerging markets, empirical studies suggest that developments in mature markets (such as greater mature market asset price volatility that reduces investors appetite for "risky assets" in general) have played a key role in reducing emerging markets' access to international capital markets.[3]

The volatility of capital flows since the mid-1990s has raised the issues of how emerging markets can achieve more stable access to international capital markets and how these economies can cope with whatever volatility does occur. While establishing sound and sustainable macroeconomic policies has been one obvious element in strengthening domestic economic fundamentals and perceived creditworthiness, many emerging markets have taken additional measures designed to "self-insure" against the volatility of capital flows and asset prices. These measures can be grouped into four general areas:
- changes in external asset and liability management practices;
- adapting exchange rate arrangements to the degree of capital account openness;
- strengthening domestic financial institutions and enhancing prudential supervision and regulation in order to increase resilience to volatility; and
- developing local securities and derivatives markets to provide an alternative source of funding for the public and corporate sectors and to facilitate the management of the financial risks associated with periods of high asset price volatility.

External Asset and Liability Management

In the period following the Asian crisis of 1997, some commentators suggested that emerging markets increase their holdings of international reserves to provide a degree of "self-insurance" against a sudden reversal of

---

[1]IMF (2003c) examines in greater detail private capital flows to emerging markets since 1990. For a discussion of the impact of volatility on income and consumption, see Prasad and others (2003).

[2]See Appendix of Chapter III of IMF (2003b) for an analysis of market closures since the mid-1990s. For analyses of sudden stops in capital flows, see Calvo (1998) and Calvo and Reinhart (2000).

[3]See Calvo (1999) and Annex III in IMF (2001). See also Chapter III of IMF (2003c) for an examination of volatility in mature markets.

Table 1. Reserves: Level and Ratio to GDP

	1990–1994 Average		1995–1999 Average		2000		2001	
	Level (In billions of U.S. dollars)	Ratio to GDP (In percent)	Level (In billions of U.S. dollars)	Ratio to GDP (In percent)	Level (In billions of U.S. dollars)	Ratio to GDP (In percent)	Level (In billions of U.S. dollars)	Ratio to GDP (In percent)
Emerging markets	**490.2**	**9.3**	**943.3**	**13.9**	**1,206.4**	**16.6**	**1,321.7**	**18.2**
Asia	**298.8**	**15.3**	**553.3**	**19.2**	**728.3**	**22.8**	**807.6**	**25.3**
of which:								
China	34.5	7.4	127.0	14.4	168.9	15.6	216.3	18.7
Taiwan Province of China	83.3	41.3	92.3	33.3	107.4	34.7	122.8	43.5
Korea	18.3	5.6	42.6	10.4	96.2	20.8	102.8	24.3
Philippines	4.0	7.4	9.5	12.5	13.4	17.9	13.8	19.3
Thailand	21.1	18.7	32.7	22.7	32.1	26.3	32.5	28.3
Malaysia	18.2	29.9	25.6	29.8	29.6	32.8	30.5	34.7
Indonesia	10.3	7.2	19.7	13.1	28.6	18.8	27.4	18.8
Latin America	**84.0**	**6.3**	**154.7**	**8.3**	**155.6**	**8.0**	**158.2**	**8.3**
of which:								
Argentina	10.0	4.6	21.2	7.4	25.1	8.8	14.6	5.4
Brazil	21.3	4.7	47.4	6.6	31.5	5.3	35.8	7.1
Mexico	15.6	4.5	25.7	6.6	35.5	6.1	44.8	7.2
Venezuela	9.7	17.5	11.9	13.7	13.6	11.2	9.7	7.7
Chile	9.1	20.1	15.3	20.0	14.7	19.7	14.2	21.4
Colombia	7.0	13.4	8.9	9.4	8.9	11.5	10.2	12.3
Peru	3.4	9.1	9.7	17.5	8.4	15.9	8.7	16.5
Europe	**31.2**	**3.8**	**101.2**	**10.0**	**132.8**	**13.8**	**145.4**	**14.5**
of which:								
Poland	4.5	5.6	21.4	14.5	26.7	16.9	25.8	14.6
Czech Republic	5.1	13.2	12.3	22.4	13.0	25.4	14.4	25.3
Hungary	4.6	12.0	10.1	21.9	11.2	24.0	10.7	20.7
Turkey	6.4	4.1	18.3	9.6	22.7	11.2	19.0	12.8
Africa	**20.4**	**5.2**	**36.8**	**8.6**	**53.1**	**12.3**	**64.7**	**15.4**
of which:								
South Africa	1.4	1.1	4.1	2.9	6.4	5.0	6.3	5.6

Source: IMF, *World Economic Outlook*.

capital flows.[4] Indeed, holdings of foreign exchange reserves by emerging markets nearly doubled between the end of 1995 and the end of 2001 (see Table 1).[5] Reserve accumulation was particularly notable for some countries that experienced "sudden stops" (or reversals) of capital flows (such as Korea, Taiwan Province of China, and Mexico).

Emerging market borrowers have also shown deftness in adapting to the volatile nature of market access.[6] In part, this has involved turning to the syndicated loan market when access to bond markets has been restricted. In addition, emerging market borrowers have attempted to develop access to the retail and institutional bond markets

---

[4]Feldstein (1999) encouraged emerging markets to accumulate reserves as insurance against the disruptive financial effects of an abrupt reversal of capital flows. According to Greenspan (1999), the Deputy Finance Minister of Argentina, Pablo Guidotti, proposed that the level of usable reserves should exceed the one-year scheduled amount of foreign currency debt amortization (assuming no rollovers). Greenspan (1999) extended Guidotti's proposal by arguing for a "liquidity-at-risk" standard that would require a country to hold liquid reserves sufficient to ensure that it could avoid new borrowing for one year with a certain ex ante probability, such as 95 percent.

[5]Moreover, the ratio of emerging markets' foreign exchange reserves to nominal GDP at the end of 2002 was at the highest level since 1990. Similar results hold for the ratios of reserves to imports and reserves to broad money (M2).

[6]The response of emerging market borrowers is analyzed more extensively in Chapter III of IMF (2001).

denominated in euros and yen when the U.S. dollar bond market has been closed. Moreover, they have employed staff in debt management agencies with extensive investment banking and trading experience, and exploited "windows of opportunity" to prefund their yearly financing requirement. They have also engaged in debt exchanges to extend the maturity of their external debt and avoid a bunching of maturities, established benchmark external bond issues both to improve secondary market liquidity and to facilitate the pricing of external corporate debt issues, and made greater use of local debt markets.

While changes in public sector external asset and liability practices have been key elements of the self-insurance response to the volatility of capital flows, the authorities in many countries have continued to use capital controls in part to affect the private sector's external asset and liability position. Indeed, the evidence for the period 1998–2000 shows that there has also been a slowdown in the removal of capital controls by countries that have had restricted capital accounts.[7] Moreover, data for 2001 do not suggest any significant change in the use of capital controls. Indeed, controls on foreign direct investment and on institutional investors rose slightly. These de jure capital controls do not necessarily provide a measure of possible changes in the de facto level of capital market integration. But they do provide a measure of the relative unwillingness of the authorities to undertake further capital account liberalization in an environment of volatile capital flows and global asset prices.

Although external asset and liability management techniques can provide a buffer against volatile capital flows and asset prices, emerging markets have also been adapting policies and the strength of their financial institutions to the degree of openness of their capital account. These adaptations have been most noticeable in the nature of exchange rate arrangements and in efforts to strengthen the ability of banking systems to withstand volatile capital flows and asset prices.

Exchange Rate Policies

While the accumulation of larger foreign exchange reserves could create more scope for the authorities to fix the exchange rate, countries have generally moved away from pegged but adjustable exchange rate arrangements since the mid-1990s, especially those with access to international capital markets.[8] For countries with access to international capital markets, the move to either a flexible exchange rate or a hard peg represents alternative solutions to the well-known problem of trying to maintain a fixed exchange rate and an independent monetary policy with a high degree of capital mobility. Moreover, it reflects the difficulties that a number of emerging markets experienced in attempting to defend a fixed exchange rate during periods of sudden stops or reversals of capital flows.

---

[7]IMF (2003a) reported, for example, that during 1998–2000, the number of countries maintaining controls on both current and capital account transactions remained relatively unchanged (falling from 74 percent to 70 percent of all IMF members). Moreover, although the overall use of capital controls did not change, a growing number of countries began to regulate selected transactions. In particular, the number of countries maintaining controls on institutional investors rose sharply. While many of these controls were prudential in nature (such as limits on purchase of foreign assets), some specified the channels' markets, and/or institutions for permitted cross-border transactions.

[8]For example, Bubula and Ötker-Robe (2002) found that between 1995 and 2001 the proportion of emerging markets with de facto floating exchange rates rose from 9 percent to 50 percent. At the same time, the proportion of countries with a hard peg also rose from 9 percent to 16 percent. This evidence is consistent with what Fischer (2001) described as the "hollowing out" of exchange rate arrangements. However, Reinhart and Rogoff (2002) argue that the shift in exchange rate arrangements has been much more complex than indicated by official classifications. Their analysis suggests that many official pegs were de facto much more flexible and conversely that many floating exchange rates showed considerable rigidity.

Financial Policies

While the changes in exchange rate arrangements removed some of the incentives for banks to borrow abroad—a major cause of the emerging market crises in the second half of the 1990s—the authorities still faced the difficulties of restructuring and recapitalizing the banks (and heavily indebted corporates), as well as ensuring that banks improve their risk management techniques amid volatile capital flows and asset prices. In short, since 1997, the results have been mixed. Asia, for example, has shown a slow but steady improvement in its soundness indicators. In contrast, Latin America witnessed an overall worsening of banking soundness, although the results vary, with countries such as Mexico and Chile continuing to improve but Argentina and Uruguay deteriorating. Central Europe has achieved the sharpest improvement in bank soundness.

Development of Local Securities and Derivatives Markets

The efforts to develop local securities and derivatives markets have been motivated by a number of considerations, especially the desire to provide an alternative source of funding in order to self-insure against capital flow reversals. Another motivation has been a desire to stimulate domestic savings by offering savers new financial instruments that broaden the set of investment opportunities and allow for better portfolio diversification. In many emerging markets, for example, domestic residents have traditionally had access to only two types of domestic instruments—bank deposits and domestic equities—and little access to international markets. Still another consideration has been to improve the intermediation of domestic savings and to attract foreign investors. This has become particularly important as a greater number of emerging markets have privatized their pension systems. In some countries, such as Chile, the private pension funds and insurance companies have been key sources of demand for high-quality corporate bonds, reflecting a desire to achieve a rate of return higher than can be obtained on bank deposits and also to obtain longer duration assets (which better match their long duration obligations). In Central Europe, foreign investors have provided a steady source of demand for sovereign bonds. Moreover, as already noted, emerging markets have also sought to develop alternative sources of funding for both the public and corporate sectors to either domestic bank lending or international capital markets.[9] In addition, local derivatives markets have been seen as providing a vehicle for managing financial risks, especially those related to exchange rates and interest rates.

Extent of Securities Market Development as an Alternative Source of Funding

Given the efforts to develop local securities markets, to what extent have these markets begun to provide an alternative source of funding to either domestic bank lending or international capital flows for both the private sector and the public sector? As will be discussed, a number of key conclusions emerge from the data on local and international issuance during the period 1997–2002. First, local corporate bond issuance has surged, particularly in Asia and Latin America. Indeed, local corporate bond issues for all emerging markets grew by nearly a factor of 10 between 1997–99 and 2000–02. Second, local bond markets have been the dominant source of

---

[9]Drawing on lessons from recent emerging markets crises, Greenspan (1999) noted that well-developed bond markets can act like a "spare tire" and substitute for bank lending as a source of corporate funding when bank lending dries up.

CHAPTER I LOCAL SECURITIES AND DERIVATIVES MARKETS IN EMERGING MARKETS: SELECTED POLICY ISSUES

Table 2. Private Sector
(In billions of U.S. dollars)

	1997	1998	1999	2000	2001	2002	1997–2002
Emerging markets[1]	325.38	253.79	174.82	401.63	295.65	476.27	1,927.54
Domestic	223.06	206.76	114.53	308.31	228.30	436.84	1,517.80
Equities	37.28	32.70	43.42	25.50	19.02	16.53	174.44
Bonds	11.17	11.70	10.47	98.01	114.47	100.61	346.42
Bank loans	174.62	162.37	60.64	184.81	94.81	319.70	996.94
International	102.32	47.03	60.30	93.32	67.35	39.42	409.74
Equities	18.42	5.59	15.76	31.90	8.81	11.01	91.48
Bonds	41.63	19.86	22.15	21.84	30.90	7.48	143.86
Bank loans	42.27	21.59	22.39	39.59	27.64	20.93	174.40
Asia	207.30	156.80	220.45	300.84	241.99	467.29	1,594.67
Domestic	154.87	144.69	193.59	245.59	198.66	443.39	1,380.78
Equities	28.11	16.69	35.52	20.65	10.76	15.35	127.08
Bonds	0.00	0.00	0.82	42.66	53.57	56.05	153.10
Bank loans	126.75	128.00	157.24	182.28	134.33	371.99	1,100.59
International	52.43	12.11	26.87	55.25	43.34	23.90	213.90
Equities	10.50	4.05	13.92	26.45	7.65	8.80	71.36
Bonds	19.60	3.41	8.24	12.45	21.50	4.01	69.21
Bank loans	22.34	4.65	4.71	16.35	14.18	11.10	73.33
Central Europe	5.51	23.14	2.91	6.76	15.34	19.29	72.95
Domestic	−0.14	18.09	−1.29	1.77	12.26	16.34	47.04
Equities	1.31	6.60	3.35	1.29	0.95	0.20	13.69
Bonds	0.50	0.28	0.33	0.17	0.32	0.07	1.68
Bank loans	−1.95	11.21	−4.97	0.31	10.99	16.07	31.67
International	5.64	5.05	4.20	4.99	3.09	2.95	25.92
Equities	2.60	1.47	1.17	0.38	0.00	0.22	5.82
Bonds	1.26	2.14	1.78	0.83	1.86	0.00	7.88
Bank loans	1.78	1.44	1.26	3.78	1.22	2.73	12.22
Latin America	112.58	73.86	−48.54	94.03	38.31	−10.32	259.92
Domestic	68.33	43.98	−77.77	60.95	17.38	−22.89	89.99
Equities	7.86	9.41	4.55	3.56	7.31	0.98	33.67
Bonds	10.66	11.42	9.32	55.17	60.58	44.49	191.64
Bank loans	49.81	23.16	−91.63	2.22	−50.51	−68.36	−135.32
International	44.25	29.87	29.23	33.08	20.93	12.57	169.93
Equities	5.33	0.07	0.67	5.07	1.16	2.00	14.30
Bonds	20.77	14.31	12.13	8.55	7.54	3.47	66.77
Bank loans	18.14	15.49	16.43	19.46	12.23	7.10	88.86

Sources: Dealogic; IMF, International Financial Statistics; S&P EMDB; and Hong Kong Monetary Authorities.
[1]Emerging markets: Argentina, Brazil, Chile, China, Czech Republic, Hong Kong SAR, Hungary, Korea, Malaysia, Mexico, Poland, Singapore, and Thailand.

funding for the public sector in all regions. Third, while emerging markets have traditionally been viewed as bank-dominated financial systems, local bond markets have become the largest single source of domestic and international funding. As already noted, this primarily reflects the heavy reliance of the public sector on bond issuance. Nonetheless, domestic corporate bond issuance rose from 4 percent of total corporate domestic and international funding in 1997–99 to 27 percent in 2000–02, whereas domestic bank credit fell from 53 percent of total corporate funding in 1997–99 to 51 percent in 2000–02.

For the private sector, Table 2 compares the domestic issuance of corporate bonds, equities, and bank lending with the issuance of international corporate bonds, equities, and syndicated loans for selected emerging markets across different regions from 1997 until 2002.[10] During this period, domestic bank lending was the dominant source of corporate funding, accounting for 52 percent of total domestic and international funding. Nonetheless, domestic corporate bond issuance rose from an annual average of $11 billion in 1997–99 to $104 billion in 2000–02; and, for the period as a whole, domestic corporate bond issues represented just under 18 percent of total funding. Domestic equity issues accounted for only about 9 percent of total funding.

International issues of bonds, equities, and syndicated loans by the corporate sector accounted for just 21 percent of total funding between 1997 and 2002 (see Table 2). However, international corporate bond issues amounted to only about 40 percent of such bonds issued domestically. Indeed, while the annual average value of domestic corporate bond issuance rose between 1997–99 and 2000–02, the annual average value of international corporate bond issuance declined from $28 billion to $20 billion. Moreover, for the entire period, international equity issuance amounted to about half of domestic equity issuance, while syndicated lending was equivalent to around 17 percent of the extension of domestic credit.

Thus, while domestic bank credit has been the primary corporate source of funding for this group of emerging markets, domestic bond markets have been an increasingly important source of funding. Indeed, domestic corporate bond issues rose from 4 percent of total corporate domestic and international funding in 1997–99 to 27 percent in 2000–02.

During the same period, domestic bank credit fell from 53 percent of total corporate funding in 1997–99 to 51 percent in 2000–02.

Between 1997 and 2002, the pattern of corporate funding revealed sharp regional differences. In Asia, domestic bank lending accounted for 69 percent of total domestic and international financing. Nonetheless, domestic bond issuance was the second largest source of corporate funding ($153 billion) and slightly exceeded corporate equity issuance ($127 billion). Indeed, domestic corporate bond issuance rose from an annual average of $275 million in 1997–99 to $51 billion in 2000–02. International issues of equity, bonds, and syndicated loans represented about 13 percent of total corporate domestic and international funding in 1997–2002.

In Central Europe, domestic bank lending was also the largest source of corporate finance during 1997–2002; but privatization helped make domestic equity issuance ($14 billion) the second largest source of funding. Domestic bond issuance remained limited.

In contrast to other regions, domestic bond issues ($192 billion) became the dominant source of corporate funding in Latin America between 1997 and 2002. Indeed, local bond issues exceeded the total of international issues of bonds, equities, and syndicated lending ($170 billion). Moreover, domestic bank lending contracted (by $135 billion).

While local securities markets have played an increasingly important role as an alternative source of funding for the domestic corporate sector, they were an even more important source of funding for the public sector (see Table 3).[11] Domestic government bond issues have clearly been the dominant source of

---

[10]The economies include China, Hong Kong SAR, Malaysia, Singapore, Korea, Thailand, Argentina, Brazil, Chile, Mexico, the Czech Republic, Hungary, and Poland. The countries were selected on the basis of the availability of data on corporate bond issuance. The data on local bond issuance cover various types of instruments, including fixed interest rate bonds, floating interest rate bonds, and bonds indexed to such items as the price level or the exchange rate. In general, it is not feasible to segment the data by type of instrument.

[11]The public sector is defined as the central government, government-owned financial institutions, and public sector enterprises.

Table 3. Public Sector[1]
(In billions of U.S. dollars)

	1997	1998	1999	2000	2001	2002	1997–2002
Emerging markets[2]	514.12	705.45	440.07	431.56	492.77	471.40	3,055.36
Domestic	452.41	662.11	399.09	386.71	456.24	442.45	2,799.02
Equities							
Bonds	387.87	626.82	383.09	357.80	395.74	421.80	2,573.12
Bank loans	64.54	35.29	16.00	28.91	60.50	20.65	225.89
International	61.71	43.33	40.98	44.85	36.53	28.95	256.35
Equities							
Bonds	41.63	28.52	34.82	32.66	29.32	20.47	187.41
Bank loans	20.08	14.82	6.16	12.19	7.20	8.48	68.94
Asia	31.58	112.02	88.27	95.18	153.75	230.35	711.15
Domestic	5.23	98.76	74.58	79.93	140.69	218.44	617.63
Equities							
Bonds	6.85	42.65	45.85	55.71	94.15	179.09	424.31
Bank loans	−1.62	56.11	28.73	24.21	46.54	39.36	193.33
International	26.35	13.26	13.69	15.25	13.06	11.90	93.52
Equities							
Bonds	14.07	6.00	9.86	7.78	10.15	7.74	55.60
Bank loans	12.28	7.26	3.83	7.47	2.91	4.16	37.91
Central Europe	39.68	55.49	59.10	54.13	78.48	52.57	339.46
Domestic	37.15	51.66	55.52	52.43	74.80	48.00	319.56
Equities							
Bonds	42.93	47.31	59.45	56.77	64.76	41.77	312.99
Bank loans	−5.77	4.35	−3.93	−4.34	10.04	6.22	6.57
International	2.53	3.83	3.59	1.70	3.68	4.57	19.90
Equities							
Bonds	1.26	2.52	2.70	1.27	2.21	3.18	13.13
Bank loans	1.26	1.31	0.89	0.43	1.47	1.40	6.76
Latin America	442.85	537.93	292.70	282.25	260.54	188.48	2,004.75
Domestic	410.02	511.69	269.00	254.35	240.75	176.01	1,861.82
Equities							
Bonds	338.09	536.85	277.79	245.31	236.84	200.94	1,835.82
Bank loans	71.93	−25.16	−8.79	9.04	3.92	−24.93	26.00
International	32.83	26.24	23.70	27.90	19.79	12.47	142.93
Equities							
Bonds	26.29	20.00	22.26	23.61	16.97	9.54	118.67
Bank loans	6.54	6.24	1.44	4.29	2.82	2.93	24.26

Sources: Dealogic; IMF, International Financial Statistics; S&P EMDB; Hong Kong Monetary Authorities; and Tesouro Nacional, Brazil.
[1]Incorporates both public sector and sovereign issuance data.
[2]Emerging markets: Argentina, Brazil, Chile, China, Czech Republic, Hong Kong SAR, Hungary, Korea, Malaysia, Mexico, Poland, Singapore, and Thailand.

funding for the public sector throughout 1997–2002. Indeed, public sector domestic bond issuance was nearly 14 times larger than international foreign currency bond issues. This primarily reflects the heavy reliance on domestic bond issuance in Latin America and, to a lesser extent, in Central Europe. Nonetheless, even in Asia, domestic bond issuance is the largest single source of public sector funding.

Despite the dominant role of domestic bond markets in all regions, the financing mix for the public sector has differed sharply across the three regions. In Asia, the public sector has relied more on credit from the banking system than in other regions.

Table 4. Total of All Sectors[1]
(In billions of U.S. dollars)

	1997	1998	1999	2000	2001	2002	1997–2002
Emerging markets[2]	839.50	959.24	614.90	833.19	788.42	947.66	4,982.91
Domestic	675.47	868.88	513.62	695.02	684.54	879.29	4,316.82
Equities	37.28	32.70	43.42	25.50	19.02	16.53	174.44
Bonds	399.04	638.51	393.56	455.80	510.22	522.41	2,919.54
Bank loans	239.15	197.66	76.64	213.73	155.30	340.35	1,222.84
International	164.03	90.36	101.28	138.17	103.88	68.37	666.09
Equities	18.42	5.59	15.76	31.90	8.81	11.01	91.48
Bonds	83.25	48.37	56.97	54.50	60.23	27.95	331.27
Bank loans	62.35	36.41	28.55	51.78	34.84	29.41	243.34
Asia	238.88	268.82	308.72	396.02	395.74	697.64	2,305.82
Domestic	160.10	243.45	268.16	325.52	339.35	661.83	1,998.41
Equities	28.11	16.69	35.52	20.65	10.76	15.35	127.08
Bonds	6.85	42.65	46.67	98.38	147.72	235.13	577.41
Bank loans	125.13	184.11	185.97	206.49	180.87	411.35	1,293.92
International	78.78	25.37	40.56	70.50	56.40	35.81	307.41
Equities	10.50	4.05	13.92	26.45	7.65	8.80	71.36
Bonds	33.67	9.40	18.10	20.24	31.65	11.75	124.81
Bank loans	34.61	11.92	8.54	23.82	17.10	15.26	111.24
Central Europe	45.19	78.63	62.02	60.89	93.82	71.86	412.41
Domestic	37.02	69.75	54.23	54.20	87.06	64.34	366.60
Equities	1.31	6.60	3.35	1.29	0.95	0.20	13.69
Bonds	43.43	47.59	59.78	56.94	65.08	41.85	314.67
Bank loans	−7.72	15.57	−8.90	−4.03	21.03	22.30	38.24
International	8.17	8.88	7.79	6.69	6.77	7.52	45.82
Equities	2.60	1.47	1.17	0.38	0.00	0.22	5.82
Bonds	2.53	4.65	4.48	2.09	4.07	3.18	21.01
Bank loans	3.05	2.76	2.14	4.22	2.69	4.13	18.98
Latin America	555.43	611.79	244.16	376.28	298.85	178.16	2,264.67
Domestic	478.35	555.67	191.23	315.30	258.14	153.12	1,951.81
Equities	7.86	9.41	4.55	3.56	7.31	0.98	33.67
Bonds	348.76	548.27	287.11	300.48	297.42	245.43	2,027.46
Bank loans	121.74	−2.01	−100.43	11.26	−46.59	−93.29	−109.32
International	77.08	56.12	52.93	60.98	40.72	25.04	312.86
Equities	5.33	0.07	0.67	5.07	1.16	2.00	14.30
Bonds	47.06	34.31	34.39	32.16	24.51	13.02	185.45
Bank loans	24.69	21.73	17.87	23.75	15.05	10.03	113.11

Sources: Dealogic; IMF, International Financial Statistics; S&P EMDB; Hong Kong Monetary Authorities; and Tesouro Nacional, Brazil.
[1]Incorporates sovereign issuance data.
[2]Emerging markets: Argentina, Brazil, Chile, China, Czech Republic, Hong Kong SAR, Hungary, Korea, Malaysia, Mexico, Poland, Singapore, and Thailand.

Moreover, the public sector in Asia met a great proportion of their financing from international sources (13 percent) than in other regions. In contrast, the public sectors in Latin America and Central Europe obtained most of their funding through domestic bond issuance (92 percent in both cases). Indeed, Latin American authorities issued over 15 times as many domestic bonds as international foreign currency bonds.

Despite the rapid expansion of local bond markets (see Table 4),[12] it remains unclear whether local securities markets have developed to the point that they will be able to

---

[12]The role of local derivatives markets in supporting both local market activities and capital flows was discussed in Chapter IV of IMF (2002d).

offset banking system weaknesses that curtail bank lending or a loss of access to international markets.[13] Moreover, emerging markets will need ongoing access to global capital markets if they are to receive the transfers of technology and capital needed for sustained growth and development. Nonetheless, the continued development of local securities and derivatives markets could eventually provide an additional "cushion" to help mitigate the most adverse effects of banking crises and/or loss of access to international capital markets by creating a longer duration domestic source of funding that may not immediately dry up when a crisis occurs and by providing some vehicles for hedging risks prior to a crisis.

Common Practices in Emerging Local Securities Markets

Given the growing importance of local securities markets as a source of funding for both the corporate and public sectors, the question arises of what policies have proven most effective in stimulating the development of these markets. Some of these common practices are briefly reviewed in this section. There is broad agreement that improvements in market infrastructure and transparency, combined with better corporate governance and the development of benchmarks and domestic institutional investors, all contribute to the development of local securities markets.

While the development of market infrastructure, institutional investors, and transparency are uncontroversial steps, countries' experience and the arguments behind some other aspects of the development of local securities markets (the "gray areas") are less clear-cut. These include the use of indexed bonds, credit risk pricing, government policies toward the development of local stock markets, the role of foreign investors, the development of local derivatives markets, and the sequencing of local securities markets reforms. Nonetheless, despite the ambiguities concerning policies in these areas, some conclusions seem warranted. For instance, the existence of indexed instruments and derivatives can contribute to lengthen and deepen fixed-income markets, but they may require careful monitoring to prevent undesirable mismatches and excessive leveraged positions. Moreover, stock market reforms that improve the conditions under which corporations issue and trade shares should be welcomed, but they should not involve the protection of local exchanges or the domestic brokerage industry from domestic or foreign competition. Similarly, foreign investors can contribute to the deepening of local markets, even if they may add to volatility during crisis episodes.

In this section, some of these common practices are briefly reviewed.[14] In the following section other selected policy issues related to the development of local securities markets (the "gray areas") are discussed.

Market Infrastructure and Benchmarks

A large number of emerging markets have improved the market infrastructure for local securities and have established relevant benchmark yield curves (see IMF, 2002b). Although the provision of a robust financial infrastructure for trading, clearing, and settlement of transactions is generally considered to be a public good, many authorities have felt that the establishment of a liquid government security benchmark yield curve in order to facilitate the pricing of corporate securities is also a desirable policy objective (see, for

---

[13]Indeed, a strong banking system is likely to play a key role in facilitating the development of local securities and derivatives since banks in emerging markets often are key underwriters of securities, investors in bonds, providers of credit to securities houses, and suppliers of over-the-counter derivative products.

[14]Surveys on some of these issues, mostly for local bond markets, include World Bank and IMF (2001); BIS (2002a); and OECD (2001).

instance, Yam, 2001). In principle, benchmarks could be provided by other instruments issued by quasi-public entities (such as the mortgage agencies in the United States) or even by private instruments (including swaps), but it is unlikely that they would reach the level of issuance and liquidity needed to perform benchmark functions.[15] In Malaysia, for instance, mortgage (Cagamas) and asset management (Khazanah) agency bonds had been used as benchmarks, but their role has recently diminished in favor of government securities. Similarly, in the Czech Republic, some corporate bonds and the swap markets have traditionally acted as benchmarks, but the small size of corporate instruments and reduced foreign participation have reduced liquidity and paved the way for the introduction of government benchmark issues.

Institutional Investors

Many emerging markets have realized the importance of developing a local institutional investor base to support local securities markets. The growth of such an investor base has usually been slow, however, and tight regulations on asset allocations have constrained the potentially beneficial role that they could bring to local securities markets.

Local pension funds have made a particularly important contribution to the development of local securities markets in Latin America and Central Europe, and their role is beginning to be felt in some of the Asian local markets. Following the lead of Chile in the 1980s, most Latin American countries have established private pension funds that have become an important source of demand for local securities, as well as for the development of market infrastructure and improved corporate governance and transparency. Similar trends are emerging in Central Europe, where mandatory private pension funds were introduced somewhat later. The provident funds systems in many Asian countries are largely under public administration and to date have not played a very active role in local market development, but some countries are gradually outsourcing funds to private asset managers.

Most countries maintain tight regulation over pension funds' asset allocations to prevent excessive risk taking and to develop local markets, but this may be a double-edged sword. Some countries restrict funds' purchases of local equities, as they are perceived as a risky investment: an extreme case is Mexico, which until recently allowed no allocation to equities. The legislation was changed in 2002 but the regulatory agency has not yet approved the implementation of the new portfolio allocations.[16] Other countries restrict the allocation to offshore instruments, seeking to develop local securities markets and to provide cheaper funds to local corporates. The recent experience in Argentina suggests, however, that local pension funds could be used as captive demand for government debt that could ultimately yield dismal returns. Indeed, in the second half of 2001, domestic holders of Argentine government bonds (primarily local pension funds and banks) were approached by the authorities to participate in a debt swap, and they were pressured into accepting new claims with lower interest rates and longer maturities.

Corporate Governance and Transparency

A number of countries have adopted measures to improve transparency and corporate governance, as they see these as critical for local capital market development. Studies

---

[15]Even in the mature markets, the low credit risk and high liquidity features of government securities have made them natural providers of benchmark interest rates (see IMF, 2001).

[16]The Mexican Congress has also approved the use of derivatives, but the pension funds still have to comply with some prudential rules and operating requirements (see Cervera and Quedry, 2003).

have shown that countries with less protection for minority shareholders have less developed equity markets and that firms in these countries use less outside finance and have higher debt-equity ratios, making them more vulnerable to shocks.[17] In response to this evidence, as well as to high-profile shareholder conflicts, some countries have recently changed the laws governing capital markets (including Brazil, Chile, the Czech Republic, and Mexico) while others (including Korea, Malaysia, Hong Kong SAR, Poland, and Singapore) have approved codes of best practice designed to improve disclosure, protect minority shareholders' rights, and maximize shareholder value.

Better corporate governance can be implemented through several mechanisms—such as improved laws, enhanced regulation and supervision, and stronger enforcement of private contracts—and, whenever changing the law has proven difficult, other mechanisms have proven to be good substitutes to some extent. A number of studies have argued that investor protection and the judicial enforcement of contracts are stronger in common-law countries than in civil law countries.[18] However, the recent experiences of Brazil and Chile, among others, show how difficult it could be to change securities laws, which generally results in substantial changes in cash flow and control rights of existing shareholders. It took the Brazilian Congress about four years to approve a new corporate law that strengthened several aspects of corporate governance in 2001, and the final legislation was watered down after protracted debates and negotiations. In particular, the law introduces a limit on the issuance of nonvoting shares (of 50 percent of total equity) only for new and nonlisted companies, but existing corporations may keep their two-thirds share of nonvoting stock even for future share issuance.[19] At the same time, the São Paulo Stock Exchange (BOVESPA) created the Novo Mercado, a new segment of the market where companies agree to the one-share-one-vote principle, allow for full tag-along rights, and enhanced corporate governance principles.

Similarly, the new capital market law in Chile establishes that any transaction between a buyer and a controlling group that would change control of the target company must be extended to remaining investors on a pro rata basis, but it leaves an opt-out option for three years.[20] Among countries perceived by market participants and academics as having relatively weak legal systems, Poland is usually cited as an example of a country where a strong stock market regulation has to a large degree acted as an effective substitute for judicial enforcement of contracts (Johnson and Shleifer, 2004).

While recent changes have improved the protection given to minority shareholders, some analysts see a risk of severely restricting the development of the market if overregulation imposes large costs on potential issuers.

---

[17]See La Porta and others (2000). Corporate governance and the development of local capital markets have been associated with macroeconomic outcomes such as output growth and the severity of exchange rate crises and output volatility (see Johnson and Shleifer, 2004, and references therein).

[18]See, for instance, La Porta and others (2000) and references therein. The authors provide measures of investor protection for 49 countries and classify them by legal origin. Besides the provision of adequate (clear and regular) information about firm performance and external audits, investor protection is usually measured by the voting rights of minorities, their ability to exercise their vote by mail and call extraordinary shareholder meetings, to participate in executive boards and have mechanisms to sue or get relief from board decisions, as well as preemptive rights to new issues and tag-along rights in the case of changes in control—to protect them from dilution by controlling shareholders.

[19]The system was devised with the aim of providing family-owned companies an incentive to list while retaining control—indeed, ownership of 17 percent of a company would ensure control. See Barham (2001).

[20]Market participants, however, doubt that many corporates will take advantage of this provision as the large pension funds may have reduced incentives to invest in an opted-out company.

Minority shareholder rights in Brazil were reduced in 1997 for macroeconomic reasons, namely to speed up and maximize the revenues from the privatization process. In a number of cases, foreign multinationals paid a premium price to obtain a controlling interest and then bought out the minorities at lower prices, but several shareholder conflicts led to the current reforms. However, some analysts worry that the government might now go too far in favoring minorities and scare away foreign investors. Similarly, a recent string of high-profile shareholder conflicts involving foreign investors in Poland has left fund managers worried that they may be seen as a threat to foreign strategic investors.[21]

Selected Policy Issues

While the development of market infrastructure, institutional investors, and transparency are uncontroversial steps, countries' experience and the arguments behind some other aspects of the development of local securities markets are less clear-cut. This section considers other selected policy issues related to the development of local securities markets, in particular those issues that could affect macroeconomic policies and/or financial stability and capital flows.

Indexed Bonds

There is broad agreement that the introduction of inflation-indexed or inflation-linked bonds provides risk-sharing opportunities for issuers and investors, and that they contribute to complete and deepen local bond markets. The issuance of inflation-linked bonds by the government is generally seen as reducing the cost to private issuers of educating investors about the benefits of these instruments as well as reducing coordination problems in the adoption of alternative units of account.

However, indexation may be difficult to reverse and foreign investors tend to shun indexed instruments. Moreover, indexation to foreign currencies—in particular, dollarization of local debt—could lead to financial instability and defeat the purpose of local debt as a self-insurance against lost access to international capital markets.

The important role of inflation-linked bonds in the development of a long-dated corporate bond market is best exemplified by the experience of Chile (see IMF, 2002b, Chapter IV). Most corporate bonds in Chile are indexed to the *Unidad de Fomento* (or UF, a unit of account linked to the Chilean consumer price index), and analysts argue that the development of a government bond market in UF, together with the adoption of a legal framework that favors (and sometimes requires) the use of such unit of account, has been central to the development of a long-term market in corporate bonds (see, for instance, Walker, 2002). To satisfy the growing demand of local institutional investors, local corporates have issued bonds with up to 30-year maturities. Although the market for indexed bonds has been in existence for more than 20 years, it has tripled in size since 2000—when the worsening of external conditions pushed corporates to issue in the local market (see Figure 1). Maturities have also been extended, from an average of 10–15 years in the first half of the 1990s, to 15–20 years more recently.

The introduction of financial indexation could complicate the achievement of monetary policy objectives and could have temporary, undesirable effects in the development of local fixed income and derivatives markets. Analysts have argued that the provision of a hedge against inflation may remove the incentives for price stability, and that financial indexation could spill over to labor contracts and increase the costs of disinflation. In the

---

[21]While most of the issues discussed in this section refer to equity markets, weak transparency and corporate governance are also a significant constraint for the development of corporate bond markets (see Sharma, 2000).

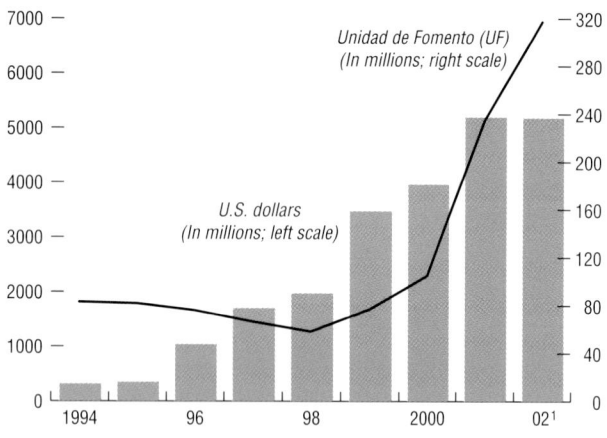

Figure 1. Chile: Amount Outstanding of Private Nonfinancial Sector Bonds

Source: Superintendencia de Valores y Seguros, Banco Central de Chile.
[1]Estimate.

case of Chile, the authorities have been trying to nominalize the short end of the curve to improve the conduct of monetary policy, but the change initially disrupted the interest rate swap market and the pricing of long-term UF instruments with maturities of less than one year.[22]

Another drawback of indexation is that foreign investors seem to dislike the complication of calculating the performance of their investments in a generally unknown unit of account. International investors, in particular pension funds and even large asset managers, seem to prefer plain vanilla bonds, where they can take a clean exposure to the currency and the underlying credit.

A large number of countries, particularly in Latin America, have managed to develop their local bond markets mostly by issuing U.S. dollar-denominated or dollar-linked debt. Analysts have offered a number of reasons for the dollarization of local bonds, some of which are of a purely macroeconomic nature and others that are related to the development of local financial markets, or even to features of the international financial system.

The standard argument against governments issuing nonindexed bonds denominated in domestic currency is that, since they also control monetary policy, they have an incentive to inflate away their debts. However, as Calvo (2000) points out, this type argument would not apply to private debt—unless the monetary authority gives more weight to the welfare of debtors compared to that of creditors. Jeanne (2002) argues that a higher share of dollarized corporate debt may be the result of a firm's optimal financial choices, when the lack of a credible monetary policy leads to high domestic interest rates. Finally, if companies expect to be bailed out by governments—especially when a pegged exchange rate is

---

[22]The nominalization of the short end of the curve has deprived the fixed-for-floating UF interest rates swap market of the reference rate for the floating leg of the transaction.

abandoned—they will tend to issue mostly dollar-denominated debt (Dooley, 2000; and Burnside, Eichenbaum, and Rebelo, 2001).[23]

The limited development of local financial markets could also be a significant factor behind the large share of dollar-denominated debt in some emerging markets. For domestic firms choosing an optimal financing mix in an uncertain operating environment, domestic currency-denominated debt could insure against low-return scenarios, especially when low returns are associated with lost or restricted access to international capital markets. However, Caballero and Krishnamurthy (2003) demonstrate that when local markets are underdeveloped and firms face credit constraints, corporates tend to underestimate the value of that insurance and issue excessive amounts of dollar-denominated debt. Firms that have good projects and could maintain access to international capital markets cannot channel resources to firms facing refinancing needs, because the latter are unable to pledge enough income to make their securities attractive to the former. More specifically, Caballero (2002) argues that the fact that large corporates moved inward to borrow in local markets during recent crises, rather than passing on their international access to smaller firms, suggests that local emerging markets remain underdeveloped and that this underdevelopment could amplify the effects of lost access to international markets.[24]

Some analysts have argued that the large share of foreign-currency-denominated emerging market debt is not just a result of weak national policies and institutions, but also a consequence of the limited incentives for currency diversification by global investors.[25] Between 1993 and 1998, four countries (the United States, the United Kingdom, Japan, and Switzerland) issued only one-third of global debt, but more than two-thirds of global debt was denominated in their own currencies. Meanwhile, developing countries issued 10 percent of global debt but had only 1 percent denominated in their own currencies. Countries belonging to the euro area show a more balanced relationship, especially after the introduction of the euro. Among the emerging markets, the share of dollar-denominated debt is smaller in the EU accession countries and highest in Latin America. Eichengreen, Hausmann, and Panizza (2002) demonstrate that standard measures of weak policies—such as high inflation—do a relatively poor job of explaining the share of dollar-denominated bonds in emerging markets, and that the only robust determinant of what the authors call "original sin" is country size. As a result, the authors claim that the solution to this problem lies not just in strengthening domestic policies and institutions but also in overcoming the difficulties created by the structure and operation of international financial markets (see Box 1).

While dollar-linked debt provides a foreign currency hedge for investors, it can lead to financial instability if the excessive use of this instrument results in sizable currency mismatches that create solvency concerns about the issuers—like the sovereign and/or non-exporters whose tax revenues or receipts are mostly denominated in local currency.[26] The

---

[23]A credible monetary policy framework and a credible commitment not to bail out debtors are obvious policy implications of these analyses.

[24]The argument applies equally to bank lending as to local bonds. Caballero and Krishnamurthy (2003) show that the limited development of local financial markets also reduces the incentives for foreign specialists—who would be willing to bring foreign capital to lend against domestic currency collateral—to enter the local market, reinforcing the underinsurance problem.

[25]Eichengreen, Hausmann, and Panizza (2002) note that transaction costs in a world of heterogeneous countries and network externalities may give a small number of vehicle currencies a special attractiveness.

[26]Similar issues arise in economies with dollarized deposits; see IMF (2003b) for a discussion of prudential and crisis management aspects of dollarized banking systems.

Box 1. An International Solution for the Original Sin

Most emerging markets cannot issue international bonds denominated in their own currencies, a fact that Eichengreen, Hausmann, and Panizza (2002) refer to as the "original sin." These economists recently proposed that the World Bank and other regional development banks sponsor a mechanism that would allow emerging markets to issue more debt denominated in their own currencies. The proposal is inspired by the fact that international financial institutions (IFIs) have issued almost half of all internationally placed bonds in exotic currencies during 1992–98. In most cases, the debt-service obligations were swapped back into U.S. dollars, providing additional support to foreign currency swap markets. The proposal involves a number of steps.

The first step would involve the development of a currency basket index that would include a well-diversified set of emerging market currencies and would contribute to overcome the relative small size of some issuers. The index would be calculated as the end-of-period exchange rate (divided by the CPI in the same month) and the weights in the index would be the countries' relative GDPs adjusted at purchasing power parity. As an illustration, the authors constructed two indices and showed that their volatility is in line with that of some major currencies and that they display a negative correlation with real private consumption growth in seven mature economies. They conclude that these characteristics of the indices would make them an attractive form of diversification for institutional and retail investors.

The next steps would have the World Bank and other IFIs issue debt denominated in the index, eventually followed by similar efforts by the Group of Ten (G-10) countries. The World Bank could also convert the U.S. dollar loans made to the countries in the index into local currency CPI-indexed loans and eliminate the currency mismatch generated by the issuance of the proposed bonds. Similarly, the authors argue that the G-10 countries could undertake currency swaps with each individual country in the index, allowing the former to eliminate the currency mismatch and providing the latter with a useful hedge against their original sin.

Finally, once a liquid market in that type of indexed debt develops, investors may want to add credit risk to the index. They could do so by buying local currency debt of the countries in the index, which will facilitate the development of these local markets.

The proposal is innovative, but analysts are skeptical about its implementation and acceptance by investors, as well as its remaining risks for the IFIs. In particular, market participants, IFI representatives, and academics are concerned that the proposal may reduce incentives to address the more fundamental issues preventing a number of emerging markets from issuing in their own currency, namely weak macroeconomic policies and related poorly developed local financial markets. In addition, potential borrowers may prefer to use their access to IFI loans in terms of foreign exchange at favorable interest rates than local currency loans. Analysts are further worried about international investors' lack of appetite for emerging markets' inflation-linked bonds. They also suggest that, despite the adjustment of the index to each of the countries' CPI, emerging markets could have an incentive to depreciate their currencies in the days before the coupons are fixed in order to lower their debt obligations. Moreover, they are concerned that the index would provide incentives to do this in a concerted fashion, creating another channel for contagion in foreign exchange markets. As a result, it may also be the case that the stronger emerging market players would not find it advantageous to participate in the index.

higher volatility of the exchange rate vis-à-vis the price level, especially during capital flow reversals, causes a deterioration in these issuers' balance sheet positions that is likely to magnify the initial problem of lost access to international capital markets and capital outflows.[27] This kind of vicious circle has meant that countries with a high degree of dollarization are likely to have more volatile output and capital flows. Indeed, Eichengreen, Hausmann, and Panizza (2002) estimate that the large share of dollar-denominated debt in emerging markets accounts for one-fourth of the difference in volatility (in GDP and capital flows) relative to mature markets.

Credit Risk Pricing

Market participants regard the lack of sophistication in pricing credit risk as a major constraint to the growth of emerging corporate bond markets. But the development of a credit culture takes time, and it is unclear how much the authorities can do to speed up this process. A few aspects of the institutional structure that could be improved include the standardization of securities contracts, the requirement of ratings, and appropriate incentives for independent securities research.

The standardization of bond contracts could contribute to a more accurate assessment of credit risk but it could also constrain the issuer's financial flexibility. In several emerging markets, bond contracts have a variety of features—coupons linked to different reference rates, embedded options and other enhancements, different types of collateral, covenants, and priority rules—that make it difficult to price the credit risk associated with the bond. Some degree of standardization and homogeneity in bond contracts would facilitate the pricing of credit risk, and securities regulators could ensure a minimum set of guidelines for such contracts. In Brazil, for instance, the authorities discussed with market participants the optimal degree of standardization, as some issuers fear that too much standardization could restrict company-specific financing needs.

Rating agencies appear to be useful in credit markets, but it is unclear to what extent regulations have to force the use of their services or whether market participants themselves would find their credit assessments useful in their pricing or allocation decisions. The requirement that local pension funds invest only in rated instruments has contributed to the development of a rather sophisticated credit risk culture in Chilean local markets. Several other emerging markets are also requiring that issuers obtain one or two ratings for their corporate bond issues. The recent Brazilian experience shows, however, that regulations do not have to be the only driving force: even though local regulations require only one rating per issue, several issuers provide two in order to reassure investors.

Finally, independent research would contribute to better credit risk assessments and pricing, but there is little the regulatory authorities can do in this area. In many emerging markets, most research available is done by the underwriters, and this could create serious conflicts of interest. This is an issue also for equities, in particular in Asian local equity markets (see, for instance, Norton, 2002; and Davies, 2002).

Local Equity Markets and the Role of Stock Exchanges

The sharp fall in domestic equity issuance in 2000–02, combined with structural developments in global equity markets, has raised doubts about the long-term prospects of

---

[27]Experience shows that the CPI is less volatile than the exchange rate, especially during crises; price indexation is also a superior alternative to indexation through floating interest rates, as the latter are also quite volatile in emerging markets.

initial public offerings (IPOs) in local markets as an alternative source of funding in emerging markets.[28] The bear market in equities has shrunk trading volumes literally everywhere and the combination of a drop in IPOs associated with the reduction in privatization and a spate of delistings has called into question the viability of many stock exchanges in emerging markets. Moreover, the competitive pressures created by declining costs—associated with automated electronic trading systems and the migration of listings toward exchanges with greater liquidity and a lower cost of funding—have stimulated both changes in stock exchange governance and increased international integration of exchanges. These developments have in turn raised the question of the proper role of the public sector in either facilitating or promoting these structural changes.

While a well-functioning stock exchange can yield efficiency gains by providing a key source of funding for the corporate sector and of liquidity for investors, there has been considerable debate about the extent of public sector involvement in helping to develop stock exchanges. There is general agreement that the development of equity markets will be facilitated by a sound macroeconomic environment, open access to foreign investors, political stability, and enforceable property rights. Properly designed and executed privatization programs can also stimulate the development of equity markets, and improvements in corporate governance and the protection of minority shareholders' interests are generally moves in the right direction.[29]

Paradoxically, the stock exchanges that have followed the best practices and have successfully developed their local markets are also encountering the highest degree of outward migration in capital raising, listing, and trading activities. However, as Claessens, Klingebiel, and Schmukler (2002) also note, migration has been beneficial in many ways: corporates have been able to raise capital at lower costs by tapping wider investor bases and investors have been able to trade shares at more liquid exchanges.[30] The authors conclude that emerging markets should focus on creating the conditions—such as improving shareholder rights and the quality of local legal systems—that allow corporations to issue and trade shares abroad in an efficient way, rather than adopt measures designed to protect local exchanges. In addition, they follow Steil (2001) and suggest that countries, especially those with small markets, should work toward having their local trading systems tightly linked or merged with global markets.

There are, however, several "gray" areas where there is much less of a consensus about the appropriate degree of official intervention.[31] One such area is the extent of corporate disclosure and accounting standards that should be mandated by the official sector. For example, Hong Kong SAR's stock exchange recently backed away from a proposal to introduce quarterly financial reporting, on the basis that it would increase companies' costs and could lead investors and management to become too focused on short-term profits—an issue also debated in some mature markets. Also, while everyone agrees that appropriate

---

[28]These concerns are particularly serious in the case of small stock markets. See IMF (2002a) for further details on domestic equity markets as a source of funding and an investment alternative for international investors. Structural issues in global and emerging equity markets are dealt with in IMF (2001).

[29]Claessens, Klingebiel, and Schmukler (2002) show that countries that follow these types of policies tend to have larger and more liquid stock exchanges. However, they also show that as such fundamentals improve, the degree of migration to other exchanges also increases.

[30]Pagano and others (2001) also show that the need for greater liquidity appears to be one of the most important factors in the decision to cross list shares and issue American Depository Receipts/Global Depository Receipts.

[31]The focus here is on structural policies. The issue of official intervention in stock and bond markets in the context of speculative attacks is dealt with in Chapter V of IMF (1999).

accounting standards should be put in place, there is considerable debate about whether these should follow Generally Accepted Accounting Principles (GAAP) or International Accounting Standards (IAS). In the end, either standard would probably work well as long as it is generally applied and enforced.

Similarly, there is no general agreement about the degree to which consumer protection and more general supervision of the exchanges should be undertaken by self-regulatory organizations (SROs) or by the authorities. While consumer protection issues (especially those related to retail investors) are often overseen by official agencies, analysts suggest that the most appropriate mix is likely to depend on the mix of local retail and institutional investors (with greater reliance on SROs when institutional investors dominate), the degree of sophistication of investors and other exchange participants, and the degree of market expertise in the official sector. Whatever mix is decided upon, it is generally agreed that regulation and supervision should not be designed to stifle competition.

Perhaps the most contentious issue in many emerging markets is the role of the authorities in promoting changes in the ownership structure of the stock exchanges, particularly from a mutual to a publicly owned corporate structure. A growing number of analysts recommend that the authorities support the demutualization of their exchanges. In many instances, this intervention is justified on the basis of a collective action problem—namely, that under a mutual ownership structure some vested interests (particularly small brokers) may block the adoption of new computer and telecommunication technologies that allow for more efficient trading platforms because such platforms would allow for more direct access to the trading floor, which could reduce brokerage revenues (see, for instance, Steil, 2001). These analysts also see a role for the official sector to help develop the telecommunication sector, especially when there are large fixed costs associated with developing such systems. However, others argue that these decisions should be left up to the exchanges themselves and that competitive pressures (especially from abroad) will bring about the necessary changes.

The Role of Foreign Investors in Local Markets

Foreign investors are an important source of demand for local securities, and several emerging markets have opened their local markets to foreign investors in an attempt to widen and diversify the investor base. Foreign participation in local equity markets appears to be larger than in local bond markets, but measurement of the latter is generally problematic and tends to underestimate foreign presence (see IMF, 2002b). Although there may be differences in investment strategies among different types of foreign investors, market participants perceive foreign investors as playing a supportive role in local markets. For instance, recent inflows to Central European countries motivated by the prospect of convergence with the European Union have been generally perceived as driven by "real money" institutional investors that have a positive long-term view on the region and contribute to the depth of local markets. Also, foreign investors usually impose positive pressure for developing robust market infrastructure and transparent market practices.

Some analysts are concerned, however, that foreign investors may be less informed than local ones and may contribute to market volatility and crises. The empirical evidence on this, however, is rather limited and inconclusive. Some argue that foreign investors seeking diversification benefits may not have an incentive to invest in the necessary information required to understand local markets and may be more prone to herding behavior; while others state that because foreign investors tend to be quite sensitive to risk and to actively manage their portfolios, they may make local markets more volatile and prone to crises. These hypotheses are difficult to test empirically and only a couple of experiences may shed light on the issue.

Analysts have suggested that it was local rather than foreign investors that were the first to leave the Mexican local market in December 1994 (see IMF, 1995; and Frankel and Schmukler, 1996). Kim and Wei (2002) examine the transactions of different types of portfolio investors in Korea before and during the Asian crisis. They find that nonresident institutional investors were always positive feedback traders, while resident investors were contrarian traders before the crisis but became positive feedback traders during the crisis.[32] Choe, Kho, and Stulz (1999) also study transaction data from the Korean stock market during the crisis and find evidence for return-chasing and herding among foreign investors before the crisis period, but no evidence for a destabilizing effect of foreign investors over the entire sample period.

Derivatives Markets

Local derivatives markets have grown in some of the large emerging markets, but notional amounts and trading volumes remain much smaller than in the mature markets.[33] The main reasons for the underdevelopment of local derivatives markets are the underdevelopment of the underlying securities markets themselves, as well as tight regulations that restrict their use by banks and investors.

Once the underlying securities markets reach a certain level of development, the efficiency gains of derivative products—in terms of unbundling and reallocating risks—become apparent and, barring regulatory obstacles, derivatives markets are likely to thrive. An example of how such gains can be achieved was recently provided in Brazil, with the unbundling of U.S. dollar-linked debt instruments into a pure local fixed-income instrument and a foreign currency swap. Investment banks in Brazil were selling U.S.-dollar-linked debt to mutual funds while simultaneously entering into two swap contracts: one that involved transferring the currency exposure to the banks—as the funds were interested in a pure fixed-income exposure—and another one that involved the sale of a dollar hedge to corporate customers that held U.S. dollar debts. To reduce the steps (and the associated intermediation spreads) involved in providing foreign exchange protection to end-users, the central bank moved to replace U.S.-dollar-linked debt with fixed-income instruments and a foreign currency swap. The changes lowered transaction costs and better accommodated the financial needs of different investors.[34]

Despite a growing acceptance that derivatives can contribute to the efficiency and stability of local financial markets, regulators in a number of emerging markets remain concerned about the potential risks involved in using instruments that have quite often been associated with financial crises. However, as noted in IMF (2002c), financial derivatives have at times magnified volatility and the effects of a financial crisis, but they were seldom the cause of the crises themselves. From the string of crises in the 1990s, it has become clear that the problem was not the use of derivatives per se, but the underlying weaknesses in domestic and global financial systems as well as shortcomings in macroeconomic policies (see also Khor, 2001). In the aftermath of crises, a large number of emerging markets have strengthened their regulatory and supervisory framework—including

---

[32]Positive feedback traders are those that buy past winners and sell past losers; negative feedback traders (or contrarians) follow the opposite trading strategy.
[33]Chapter IV in IMF (2002c) presents estimates of the size of emerging derivatives markets.
[34]By end-December 2002, U.S.-dollar-linked debt had fallen to $40 billion (from $77 billion the previous year), while the level of swaps outstanding had reached $26 billion.

SELECTED POLICY ISSUES

for the use of derivatives. Market participants note that in some markets the main constraint to the development of onshore derivatives markets is not the legislation, but the regulators' concern about the lack of knowledge and understanding of the products (see, for instance, Ransley, 2002).

Analysts also note that there are risks related to the nonexistence of hedging instruments, or to the fact that they may be developed offshore. For instance, the recent rapid expansion of local bond markets was supported by a low interest rate environment, and some market participants are concerned that investors may not have instruments available to hedge against any reversal in the interest rate cycle. Derivatives bring together hedgers and speculators that normally tend to increase the liquidity and smooth price changes in the underlying securities. Problems arise when the market becomes one-sided, as in Brazil's foreign exchange market by mid-2002, when the only supplier of foreign exchange hedge was the sovereign itself.[35] Similarly, as the experience with equity markets demonstrates, if capital controls or other regulatory obstacles send markets offshore, it may be difficult to reverse the flow and develop the onshore markets.

The possibility that the rapid growth of derivatives may outstrip the risk management capabilities of end users and the supervisory capabilities of regulatory authorities is nevertheless a legitimate concern. Regulators, therefore, have to strike a balance between the need to allow for better risk management and market development and the risk of increased exposure to potential vulnerabilities. The first line of defense against the latter is sound and credible macroeconomic policies. The second line of defense is policies geared toward enhanced risk management capabilities of financial institutions, combined with up-to-date risk assessment capabilities of regulators. Both kinds of measures point to the need to foster transparency and prompt disclosure of relevant information. A number of emerging markets have strengthened financial regulation and adopted Basel-type guidelines for capital adequacy—including for derivative instruments—and this would go a long way toward preventing and mitigating derivatives-related vulnerabilities. Frequent contact with market participants and the discussion and consultation of regulatory changes with the industry are also useful for the early detection of these vulnerabilities. Finally, investor protection arguments suggest that, even if retail investors' exposures are not large, efforts should be made to clarify the nature of risks associated with different instruments, either through warnings in the contracts or other means of investor education.

Sequencing

The development of local securities markets raises a number of interesting questions about the optimal sequencing vis-à-vis the development of other financial markets and institutions—such as money markets and banks—as well as other macroeconomic and regulatory policies. Broadly speaking, a comparison of different types of financial systems, and their evolution over time, is a complex issue and there are no simple answers to what would be an optimal development strategy (see Allen and Gale, 2000). Nevertheless, a gradual and complementary approach is beneficial as a general rule, though in some cases, a given sequencing may be preferable.

Some analysts suggest that it may be optimal to develop first a deep local debt market before opening up the capital account. An example of the former strategy is the path followed by Australia (see Eichengreen and

---

[35]The availability of derivative instruments and markets to trade them should not be confused with the availability of an abundant supply of "hedge"—the latter being related to the credibility of macroeconomic policies and the willingness to take one side of the market.

Hausmann, 1999), which has developed a deep local bond market and has some 44 percent of its external debt denominated in local currency.[36] This seems to be the path chosen by two large emerging markets—China and India—that have sizable local debt markets and have not yet fully opened up to foreign investors (see IMF, 2002b; and BIS, 2002a). The potential benefits of developing local markets in isolation from international markets have to be weighed against traditional arguments against capital controls (such as misallocation of resources, increased costs of funding, and evasion; see Dooley, 1996), as well as the fact that market participants argue that controls have in some instances reduced liquidity and hence hindered the development of local securities markets.[37]

Developing external debt markets may also have positive benefits for the development of local securities markets, as firms that access international markets learn issuance techniques that can be transferred later on to their local issuance programs. Countries such as Chile and Mexico have developed first an external bond market for the sovereign, which was then followed by the corporate sector, and afterwards used that experience to grow their local markets.[38] The development of an external debt market may also help in mitigating one particular downside of an exclusive reliance on local debt markets. That is, in the event of a debt restructuring, the existence of an external debt market makes possible the transfer of a part of the costs of restructuring to nondomestic entities. In particular, this can minimize disruptions associated with banking crises, when domestic banks are a significant holder of a sovereign's debt.

The development of well-functioning money markets appears to be a critical first step in developing corporate bond markets (see Schinasi and Smith, 1998), as well as derivatives markets. Money markets provide an anchor to the short end of the yield curves and are critical for the pricing of fixed-income securities and derivatives. Korea and Thailand provide examples of the difficulties of developing a secondary bond market and the associated derivatives markets without the support of a money market (see Cha, 2002; and IMF, 2002b).

Although local securities markets can provide an alternative source of funding to the banking sector, especially during banking crises (Greenspan's "spare tire"), a sound and well-regulated banking system can be a necessary complement to the development of local securities markets. Banks can play a number of supporting roles for securities markets: they can be large holders of securities, underwriters and market makers, issuers, and guarantors, as well as arrangers of securitizations (see Hawkins, 2002). The large involvement of banks in the securities business requires appropriate regulations ("firewalls") to prevent the issuance of bonds to repay loans and subsequent sale of the bonds to an asset manager subsidiary at higher-than-market prices. Banking and bond markets could be developed in tandem, building an appropriate regulatory and institutional framework to encompass both.

Finally, local securities markets remain highly segmented in most regions, and a number of measures would have to be undertaken to develop fully integrated, regional markets. Despite their recent growth and deepening, Asia's domestic currency bond markets, for instance, are largely insulated from each other. Domestic investors in several countries are not allowed to invest in international markets, and foreign investors are not attracted by the low yield and costly hedges. Analysts note

---

[36]The authors caution, however, against attempts to follow this path—namely to reverse the opening of the capital account—for countries that have followed alternative sequencing strategies.

[37]Chile is sometimes mentioned as an example; see Cifuentes, Desormeaux, and Gonzalez (2002).

[38]Yuan (2000) shows that issuance of sovereign bonds in international markets creates informational externalities that improve the liquidity of corporate bonds.

that, besides the removal of controls and harmonization of taxes, several institutional aspects of bond markets—such as contracts, underwriting, and settlement conditions—would have to be standardized to some extent before a pan-Asian market could be created (see, for instance, Parsons, 2001). However, a series of overlapping proposals to develop a regional bond market in the region may focus the authorities' efforts on the removal of some of these barriers and contribute to speed up the process.[39]

Conclusion

Local securities and derivatives markets have grown substantially over the last five years. Despite the rapid expansion of local markets—in particular, local bond markets—they have not yet developed enough to provide full insurance against the closure of banking or international markets. Nonetheless, continued efforts to develop these markets could eventually provide a significant cushion against future closures. In particular, these efforts should focus on continuing to adopt measures geared toward strengthening market infrastructure, developing benchmarks and local institutional investors, and improving corporate governance and transparency. Moreover, despite the existence of ambiguities concerning some policies (the "gray areas") related to the development of local securities and derivatives markets, several measures could still be undertaken, while monitoring and controlling their potentially negative side effects. For instance, well-developed derivatives markets provide efficient instruments for risk management, and experience shows that sound macroeconomic and regulatory policies can largely mitigate their potentially negative effects on financial stability. Similarly, indexed instruments contribute to increase duration in fixed-income markets, but excessive indexation to foreign exchange could lead to balance sheet mismatches and unstable debt dynamics and, hence, should be discouraged.

---

[39]These include work aimed at developing local bond markets by APEC, the ASEAN+3 group, and a recent proposal by the Asian Cooperation Dialogue (ACD). The latter would involve a set of Asian governments launching a regional bond fund, financed by Asian central banks, that would "catalyze" larger investments from institutional investors and would invest initially in U.S. dollar, euro, and other nonregional currency bonds, later diversifying into local currency bonds from government and corporate issuers.

CHAPTER II EMERGING LOCAL BOND MARKETS

Jorge E. Roldos

A key policy prescription for fending off financial crises in emerging markets has been the development of local bond markets, and this strategy has been embraced by a number of policymakers and international organizations (see World Bank and IMF, 2001). From a macroeconomic perspective, local bond markets could soften the impact of lost access to international capital markets or bank credit by providing an alternative source of funding.[40] From a microeconomic perspective, they could help create a wider menu of instruments to deal with inherent currency and maturity mismatches in emerging markets (see Eichengreen and Hausmann, 1999; and HKMA, 2001).

In part as a result of the implementation of this policy prescription, emerging local bond markets have grown considerably over the past five years, and they are gradually becoming an alternative source of funding for both sovereigns and corporates. Also, as it becomes easier to invest across borders, local instruments are also attracting the interest of global fixed-income investors. In this chapter, we assess recent trends in emerging local bond markets, with particular attention to how they relate to global bond markets and international capital flows.

Size and Structure of Global Bond Markets

The size of global bond markets reached $43 trillion by the end of 2002, and overall the issuance of international bonds has expanded relative to domestic issuance. Indeed, international bonds constitute 20 percent of the global market, compared to 11 percent in 1997. Moreover, cross-border trading of bonds has become a key component of international capital flows (see Merrill Lynch, 2001). While such cross-border trading has affected emerging as well as mature markets, foreign participation in local emerging bond markets remains limited. Nonetheless, global bond fund managers have recently shifted their global benchmarks away from pure government indices, and are increasingly looking at investment opportunities in emerging bond markets (see *Emerging Markets Investor*, 2001).

Emerging bond markets have been growing faster than other bond markets, but so far they are just 6 percent of the global market (Table 5). Although foreign investors have tended to focus on foreign currency external debt issued by emerging markets, the size of the local bond markets is four times as large (i.e., $1,980 billion versus $512 billion of external bonded debt; see Table 5).

The structure of emerging bond markets as a whole is similar to that of the mature markets, with around two-thirds of bonds issued by governments and financial institutions, and the rest distributed between corporate (around 10 percent) and international bonds (around 20 percent, Table 5). There are, however, some notable regional differences. While Latin American markets are dominated by domestic government and international bonds (47 and 39 percent of the total, respectively), Asian bond markets have a larger share of corporate bonds (18 percent; even

---

[40]See Greenspan (1999). However, while bond markets and banks have served as backup forms of financial intermediation in the United States, empirical evidence for a broader set of countries shows a positive correlation between bank lending and bond issuance—see Hong Kong Monetary Authority, HKMA (2001).

Table 5. Size and Structure of the Global Bond Market in 2002
(Nominal value in billions of U.S. dollars)

Country	Total Bond Outstanding	Percent of World Bond Market	Domestic Government[1] Billions of U.S. dollars	Percent of total	Financial institutions Billions of U.S. dollars	Percent of total	Corporate Billions of U.S. dollars	Percent of total	International[2] Billions of U.S. dollars	Percent of total
United States	19,014.7	44.5	4,529.5	23.8	9,323.9	49.0	2,419.2	12.7	2,742.1	14.4
Euro area[3]	10,042.1	23.5	3,828.1	38.1	2,162.4	21.5	492.2	4.9	3,559.4	35.4
Japan	7,005.1	16.4	4,837.5	69.1	1,157.8	16.5	752.7	10.7	257.1	3.7
Other mature markets	4,193.2	9.8	1,275.3	30.4	927.6	22.1	466.2	11.1	1,524.1	36.3
Subtotal	**40,255.1**	**94.2**	**14,470.4**	**35.9**	**13,571.7**	**33.7**	**4,130.3**	**10.3**	**8,082.7**	**20.1**
Emerging Markets										
Asia	1,541.0	3.6	645.3	41.9	419.0	27.2	274.2	17.8	202.5	13.1
Latin America	594.1	1.4	280.4	47.2	57.7	9.7	26.5	4.5	229.5	38.6
Eastern Europe, Middle East, Africa	356.5	0.8	256.3	71.9	12.7	3.6	8.0	2.2	79.5	22.3
Subtotal	**2,491.6**	**5.8**	**1,182.0**	**47.4**	**489.4**	**19.6**	**308.7**	**12.4**	**511.5**	**20.5**
Total	**42,746.7**	**100.0**	**15,652.4**	**36.6**	**14,061.1**	**32.9**	**4,439.0**	**10.4**	**8,594.2**	**20.1**

Source: Staff estimates based on BIS Statistical Tables on Securities.
[1]Since 2002 BIS has reclassified data on bonds issued by government agencies to public financial institutions and public corporate issuers as appropriate.
[2]Includes bonds issued by governments, financial institutions, and corporates in international markets.
[3]Euro area includes a total of 11 members of the euro zone, excluding Luxembourg.

larger than the 13 percent in the United States) and a relatively smaller share of international bonds. The rest of the emerging market universe is also dominated by government bonds, with 72 percent of the total market—a share comparable to that of the Japanese bond market.

Local Bond Markets as an Alternative Source of Funding

The rapid growth of emerging local bond markets over the last five years has been a natural outcome of financial crises. It also stems from the desire of governments, banks, and corporates to substitute domestic for external sources of finance to protect themselves against the on-off nature of access to international capital markets.

Until the mid-1990s, emerging local bond markets were generally underdeveloped, with restricted demand for fixed-income products, a limited supply of quality bond issues and inadequate market infrastructure. However, particularly in the period after the Asian crisis, many governments have made determined efforts to overcome these limitations. Nonetheless, there are regional differences in how rapidly the markets have developed. In Asia, the growth of local bond issuance has been driven by the need to recapitalize banking systems and more recently to finance expansionary fiscal policies. The lack of bank credit has also contributed to some increase in corporate bond issuance, not just in Asia but also in Latin America. In the latter region, the rapid growth of local institutional investors has driven the growth of local bond markets, together with large refinancing needs of the corporate sector in a difficult external environment. Finally, the buildup of institutions—such as debt management agencies—and the harmonization of regulations in the process of accession to the European Union have contributed to the growth of these markets in the Czech Republic, Hungary, and Poland—the so-called CE-3 countries.

A number of countries have made substantial progress in the development of government bond markets, but progress has been slower in corporate bond markets.[41] While this has been the sequence of market development observed in many countries, there is nevertheless a risk that improved bond markets and debt management strategies could lead to excessive government debt issuance and crowding out of the corporate sector.

Government Bond Markets

While the increased issuance of government bonds has primarily reflected the financing of fiscal imbalances, there have been cases where governments have engaged in deliberate efforts to develop debt markets even without immediate fiscal needs. A large number of emerging markets have adopted debt management policies aimed at ensuring that "the government's financing needs and its payment obligations are met at the lowest cost over the medium to long run, consistent with a prudent degree of risk" (see World Bank and IMF, 2001). A secondary but sometimes equally prominent objective has been the development of the bond market through a number of policy initiatives. These initiatives have included increasing market depth and transparency through preannounced and regular issuance programs, establishing benchmark issues and yield curves, improving market infrastructure, and developing a local investor base. In addition, some countries, such as Chile, Hong Kong SAR, and Singapore, have also made efforts to develop their bond markets even in the absence of explicit fiscal needs.

Increasing Market Depth and Establishing Benchmark Issues

Significant progress has been made in the development of local bond markets in Asia, with most progress concentrated in the government bond segment. In Thailand, for instance, the outstanding value of the total bond market has increased from 10 percent of GDP in 1996 to 37 percent of GDP by the end of 2002, with the largest increase in the government bond segment. The ministry of finance has established and announced a regular program for government bond and treasury bill issuance, with maturities ranging from 1 to 20 years. Similarly, the outstanding stock of government bonds increased by more than 10 percent of GDP in 1998 in both Korea and Malaysia (to 16.1 and 31.5 percent of GDP, respectively; see Table 6), and have continued to grow. Both markets continue to be dominated by corporate bonds, but governments have also made recent efforts to develop benchmark yield curves. Before 1998, market participants used three-year guaranteed corporate bonds as benchmarks in Korea, but since then the authorities have increased issuance and unified several issues into standardized treasury bonds that are currently issued up to 10-year maturities. Despite government efforts to develop a benchmark curve, market participants note that establishment of the curve in Malaysia has been complicated by the plurality of contenders for the title of "government bond" (see Moody's, 2002).

China's government local bond market has grown in a remarkably short period of time to become the largest in the region (excluding Japan). The total outstanding of treasury bonds reached 20 percent of GDP in 2001 and it declined somewhat in 2002, but the stock of tradable bonds has continued to rise. In 2001, the treasury added 15-year and 20-year bonds to the existing stock. The government has a quarterly issuance calendar, and around 50 institutions participate in the auctions. More recently, the authorities have announced that they may use the local bond

---

[41]As in previous reports, only a select sample of emerging markets is covered in this chapter. These countries are those that have been visited by the staff in the past two years, and where information on recent developments is most up-to-date.

Table 6. Selected Emerging Local Bond Markets: Amounts Outstanding
(In percent of GDP)

		1994	1995	1996	1997	1998	1999	2000	2001	2002
Emerging Markets	**Domestic Bonds**	**23.3**	**24.9**	**26.4**	**24.9**	**33.6**	**35.5**	**35.1**	**38.8**	**40.3**
	Governments	*11.5*	*12.0*	*13.5*	*14.1*	*17.9*	*19.4*	*19.7*	*22.0*	*21.4*
	Corporate sector	*3.1*	*3.5*	*3.8*	*2.9*	*4.6*	*5.3*	*5.2*	*5.7*	*6.6*
	Financial institutions	*8.7*	*9.3*	*9.1*	*7.9*	*11.1*	*10.8*	*10.3*	*11.1*	*12.3*
Asia	Domestic Bonds	26.0	26.6	27.2	22.3	36.7	39.9	40.5	44.7	47.2
	Governments	8.3	8.1	8.2	7.3	12.4	15.0	16.0	18.3	18.8
	Corporate sector	5.9	6.3	6.7	4.7	8.4	8.8	8.5	9.2	10.0
	Financial institutions	11.8	12.2	12.2	10.3	15.8	16.1	15.9	17.3	18.4
China	Domestic Bonds	12.2	13.3	14.6	18.0	24.1	29.5	32.9	34.8	33.3
	Governments	4.7	5.6	6.4	7.5	10.1	13.0	15.3	17.4	16.3
	Corporate sector	0.7	0.6	0.5	0.7	0.9	0.9	1.0	0.9	0.8
	Financial institutions	6.7	7.1	7.7	9.8	13.2	15.6	16.6	16.5	16.2
Hong Kong SAR	Domestic Bonds	12.5	16.8	21.5	23.7	24.1	26.5	25.8	26.6	27.4
	Governments	5.1	5.4	7.6	7.5	7.7	8.2	8.4	8.9	9.3
	Corporate sector	1.3	1.8	1.7	2.0	1.8	3.0	3.0	3.0	2.9
	Financial institutions	6.2	9.6	12.2	14.2	14.7	15.4	14.5	14.6	15.2
Malaysia	Domestic Bonds	72.0	70.2	72.5	56.9	85.8	83.5	83.0	94.4	86.9
	Governments	42.2	36.5	29.9	19.4	31.5	31.2	31.4	36.3	35.7
	Corporate sector	15.3	17.6	23.3	20.8	33.8	43.2	45.3	47.9	39.9
	Financial institutions	14.5	16.2	19.2	16.8	20.5	9.1	6.2	10.0	11.1
Singapore	Domestic Bonds	28.6	27.6	27.0	25.2	34.5	43.3	45.4	59.3	63.8
	Governments	15.8	15.8	16.1	13.9	20.2	25.1	26.3	32.9	36.3
	Corporate sector	0.0	0.0	0.0	2.5	3.1	4.3	4.5	6.5	6.8
	Financial institutions	12.9	11.8	10.8	8.9	11.1	14.1	14.5	19.9	20.7
Korea	Domestic Bonds	46.0	46.4	45.9	27.3	75.7	65.4	58.3	69.3	82.5
	Governments	8.9	8.4	8.4	5.3	16.1	17.9	15.9	18.3	20.7
	Corporate sector	15.1	16.2	17.4	11.2	32.1	25.9	23.0	27.8	32.8
	Financial institutions	22.0	21.8	20.1	10.9	27.4	21.6	19.3	23.2	29.0
Thailand	Domestic Bonds	9.6	9.2	9.6	6.3	21.1	25.7	25.4	31.4	37.4
	Governments	1.7	1.0	0.4	0.2	10.1	13.3	13.6	16.0	22.9
	Corporate sector	2.1	2.1	2.8	1.9	3.0	3.9	4.0	4.9	5.1
	Financial institutions	5.8	6.1	6.4	4.2	8.0	8.5	7.8	10.5	9.4
Latin America	Domestic Bonds	20.7	23.3	26.3	28.7	31.7	31.3	29.5	32.1	28.7
	Governments	13.6	15.7	19.1	21.6	22.9	24.5	23.5	25.9	22.2
	Corporate sector	0.6	0.5	0.6	1.0	1.1	1.4	1.6	1.7	2.0
	Financial institutions	6.5	7.1	6.5	6.0	7.7	5.4	4.4	4.5	4.5
Argentina	Domestic Bonds	11.6	10.0	10.7	11.7	13.4	15.0	16.5	13.9	25.2
	Governments	8.9	7.7	7.8	7.6	8.7	10.1	11.6	9.1	12.2
	Corporate sector	1.1	1.2	1.3	1.9	2.4	2.6	2.6	2.7	8.4
	Financial institutions	1.7	1.1	1.7	2.3	2.3	2.3	2.3	2.0	4.6
Brazil	Domestic Bonds	31.7	32.9	38.2	42.6	49.8	56.1	49.7	61.2	47.2
	Governments	18.6	21.3	28.0	32.7	36.5	45.5	41.5	51.3	38.0
	Corporate sector	0.0	0.0	0.1	0.6	0.3	0.4	0.6	0.5	0.4
	Financial institutions	13.1	11.5	10.1	9.4	13.0	10.1	7.7	9.3	8.8
Chile	Domestic Bonds	43.9	39.7	42.6	44.2	42.6	45.2	46.6	52.2	52.9
	Governments	30.0	26.2	27.8	29.1	26.6	27.9	28.3	28.4	29.0
	Corporate sector	4.4	3.3	3.0	2.3	2.9	3.6	4.8	9.2	9.9
	Financial institutions	9.4	10.0	11.7	12.8	13.1	13.7	13.3	14.6	14.0
Mexico	Domestic Bonds	8.8	7.7	7.3	9.6	8.9	11.8	12.7	14.2	13.9
	Governments	7.7	6.3	5.7	7.9	7.1	9.6	10.1	12.0	12.0
	Corporate sector	0.6	0.6	0.5	1.0	1.2	1.3	1.8	1.5	1.3
	Financial institutions	0.6	0.8	1.0	0.7	0.6	0.9	0.8	0.7	0.6

Table 6 *(concluded)*

		1994	1995	1996	1997	1998	1999	2000	2001	2002
Eastern Europe	Domestic Bonds	21.6	21.3	21.1	20.7	25.0	26.1	27.5	30.7	38.6
	Governments	20.7	19.9	19.4	18.7	23.0	23.8	25.0	28.5	36.1
	Corporate sector	0.3	0.5	0.7	1.0	0.9	1.1	1.3	1.2	1.3
	Financial institutions	0.6	0.9	1.0	1.1	1.1	1.1	1.2	1.0	1.2
Czech Republic	Domestic Bonds	17.5	23.3	21.5	23.6	39.3	45.5	45.5	45.4	61.0
	Governments	14.1	17.5	14.6	15.9	31.2	36.4	34.8	36.2	51.8
	Corporate sector	1.0	1.9	2.6	3.2	3.3	4.4	5.2	4.8	4.6
	Financial institutions	2.7	3.8	4.2	4.5	4.7	4.7	5.4	4.6	4.7
Hungary	Domestic Bonds	28.9	26.4	33.4	30.6	33.6	34.6	35.4	37.9	48.3
	Governments	28.4	25.7	32.8	28.4	32.1	32.7	33.3	35.6	45.8
	Corporate sector	0.2	0.4	0.4	1.5	1.1	1.2	1.5	1.5	1.7
	Financial institutions	0.2	0.2	0.2	0.7	0.4	0.6	0.6	0.8	0.8
Poland	Domestic Bonds	20.2	18.8	17.2	16.7	17.6	16.9	19.6	24.2	27.1
	Governments	20.2	18.8	17.2	16.7	17.6	16.9	19.6	24.2	27.1
	Corporate sector	0.0	0.0	0.0	0.0	0.0	0.0	0.0	0.0	0.0
	Financial institutions	0.0	0.0	0.0	0.0	0.0	0.0	0.0	0.0	0.0

Sources: Bank for International Settlements; and IMF staff estimates.

market to finance the restructuring of the banking sector.

For governments that have consistently run fiscal surpluses, the development of the local bond market involves a series of costs, especially when there are few high-return uses for the funds raised. The Hong Kong SAR authorities nonetheless argue that public-good aspects of bond markets justify some degree of official involvement in their development—in particular those related to market infrastructure (see Yam, 2001), and the Singapore authorities appear to have been willing to incur costs related to the development of a government yield curve under the belief that the benefits of becoming a regional bond center dominate the implied costs.[42]

Both financial centers have undertaken explicit measures to help develop the market. The Hong Kong dollar bond market was one of the first domestic bond markets to develop in Asia, and it has grown from 13 percent of GDP in 1994 to 27 percent of GDP in 2002 (Table 6). The HKMA has established a government bond curve up to 10 years through the Exchange Fund Notes and Bills program, but issuance is limited by the currency board arrangement and ample fiscal reserves. Given the limited size of the outstanding issues, some market participants argue that the interest rate swap curve constitutes a more liquid benchmark. Singapore has taken a much more proactive approach to develop the bond market and accelerated the issuance of Singapore Government Securities (SGS): the outstanding amount has doubled from 14 percent of GDP in 1997 to 36 percent of GDP in 2002. In August 1998, the Monetary Authority of Singapore began issuing 10-year SGS and in September 2001 it extended the yield curve to 15 years. Meanwhile, issue size has been increased to around 2.5 billion Singapore dollars (US$1.5 billion) and the monetary authority has conducted bond purchase operations to rechannel liquidity from small-size, off-the-run SGS issues into larger benchmark bonds. As a result of these efforts, in April 2001, Singapore became the first Asian country outside Japan to be included in J.P. Morgan's Global Bond Index.

---

[42]As yields in Singapore Government Securities (SGS) have generally been lower than those of G-7 securities, the costs of developing the market—including those of managing securities issuance and operating the SGS trading system—are likely to have been rather small.

The growth and deepening of government bond markets in the CE-3 countries has been supported by strong institutional development, in particular by the early establishment of public debt management agencies. For example, the Government Debt Management Agency of Hungary (AKK) and the public debt department of Poland's ministry of finance have pursued issuance strategies aimed at minimizing their exposure to foreign exchange and rollover risks,[43] while developing local government bond markets. In the local market, Poland's issuance strategy has been designed to increase the liquidity and extend the maturity of the treasury securities market, but it has also been required to adjust to budgetary pressures. Issuance of existing series of securities has been increased at the expense of the introduction of new series, the number of auctions has been reduced, and reverse auctions have been recently introduced to increase the size of key benchmark issues. Despite plans to lengthen the maturity structure of government securities, budgetary pressures and successive reductions in short-term interest rates led to an increase in the issuance of treasury bills in the second half of 2001, and the share of such instruments in total debt increased to 18 percent by the end of 2001 from 16 percent in December 2000. However, this was countered by the sovereign's recent issuance of the first 20-year local bond from the region.

Hungary's AKK has been instrumental to the development of a liquid government debt market and has recently focused its issuance strategy on smoothing the transition from a forint-denominated debt market to a euro-denominated debt market. The agency realizes that the separation of the external and domestic debt markets will become redundant with the adoption of the euro. As a result, market practices have been brought in line with those of the euro zone—including price calculations, quotations, and the use of annual coupon payments. The agency has also continued to lengthen the maturity of government debt and this has been reflected in the recent issuance of a 15-year forint-denominated bond.

The Czech Republic also extended the government local yield curve to 15 years in January 2001. However, treasury bills with maturities of up to one year still form over one-half of the government debt, which increases rollover risk at a time when the deficit is about 5 percent of GDP.

In Latin America, Brazil had the largest and fastest growing government bond market until 2001: domestic public debt had grown from 33 percent of GDP in 1997 to 51 percent in 2001 (Table 6). By the end of 2001, the total amount of public debt amounted to $325 billion (65 percent of GDP), of which $270 billion corresponded to domestic bonds and $55 billion to external bonds. The authorities have undertaken a series of measures to improve the conduct of public debt management, but macroeconomic instability has hampered efforts to build up a benchmark yield curve. The main focus in terms of risk management has been the avoidance of refinancing risks. In this respect, the authorities have successfully extended the average maturity of the domestic debt—from around 10 months in 1999 to 35 months at the end of 2001—and have achieved a smoother redemption profile, with the share of debt maturing in 12 months falling to 26 percent of the total by the end of 2001, compared with 53 percent in 1999. However, the objective of lower refinancing risk was achieved at the expense of higher market and credit risk, as investors required indexation to overnight interest rates and exchange rates to extend maturities. The resulting increase in indexed debt (see Box 2),

---

[43]As a result of this strategy, foreign currency debt as a percent of total government securities declined from 53 percent in 1997 to 42 percent in 2001 in Poland, and from 41 percent to less than 30 percent in Hungary in the same period.

Box 2. Indexed Bonds

Indexed bonds are becoming more popular among investors and issuers in the mature markets, but they have a long history in inflation-prone emerging markets (see Merrill Lynch, 2002). The development of inflation-indexed (or inflation-linked, IL) bonds in the mature markets started with the introduction of IL Gilts in the United Kingdom in 1981, in response to highly volatile and negative real returns experienced by pension funds. A number of other mature markets for indexed bonds developed in the 1980s and 1990s, with the United States and France the latest to join in 1997 and 1998, respectively. However, IL bonds became popular in high inflation emerging markets during the 1970s, prompting a debate of the costs and benefits of such instruments that still continues.

The discussion of the costs and benefits of IL bonds indexation is usually focused on the macroeconomic consequences of indexation, but the issue also has important implications for financial markets. Proponents of IL bonds argue that they may lower the cost of funding for the government and that they provide information on inflation expectations and incentives for governments to keep inflation down. Detractors of IL bonds make the case that indexation of financial assets may spill over to labor markets and contribute to make inflation more persistent and costly. However, there is almost a consensus that IL bonds provide risk-sharing opportunities to investors and issuers alike, and that they contribute to complete asset markets in an efficient way. There is less agreement though on what role the government should have in the provision of such contracts, but a case can be made for the government to publish and coordinate the use of an IL unit of account to be used in such contracts (see, for instance, Campbell and Shiller, 1996).

Recent experiences in Latin America provide some useful insights on the costs and benefits of IL bonds, as well as on other aspects of indexation. In particular, they show that indexation could help deepen and lengthen both private and public bond markets, but that they need to be complemented with stable macroeconomic policies and capital market reforms that favor the creation of a large institutional investor base.

The creation of the *Unidad de Fomento* (UF), an indexed unit of account, together with the development of a strong institutional investor base, has played a central role in the development of the local Chilean bond markets. In particular, most corporate bonds in Chile are indexed to the UF, and this contributed to the recent growth of the corporate bond market, as well as to the long maturities achieved in local currency bonds. Local corporates generally issue bonds in two tranches, one of five to eight years, targeted to pension funds, and another of 20 years or more, targeted to insurance companies. Tight regulations on asset and liability management for insurance companies have generated demand for long-dated paper, and issuers have gone up to 30 years. Analysts argue that, had it not been for the required use of the UF for many financial contracts and for the development of a UF-denominated government bond market, the fixed income market would have developed toward shorter-term, dollar-denominated securities (see Walker, 2002).

In Brazil, efforts to deindex the stock of domestic debt during the successful Real Plan of 1994–98 led to a relatively large share of fixed-rate debt (approximately 60 percent of the total) by mid-1997. However, increased instability in the wake of the 1998–99 financial crisis reduced drastically the share of fixed-rate bonds, and the authorities had to increase the supply of bonds indexed to the overnight interest rates and the U.S. dollar in order to reduce refinancing risk. Also, the authorities did not want to lock in high real interest rates or undo the deindexation (to inflation) achieved during the Real Plan. As a result, IL bonds have regained

> importance only gradually, and most of the rest of the financial system is indexed to overnight interest rates.[1]
>
> [1]IL bonds were around 12 percent of total government debt in 2002, compared to 20 percent in the United Kingdom.

> Only recently a market for inflation-linked corporate bonds has reached volumes that are still a fraction (in terms of GDP) of those seen in Chile, in maturities of three to six years.

combined with money and foreign exchange market pressures, has led to a complicated debt dynamics that was associated with a shortening of maturities by mid-2002. Indeed, as concerns about political developments intensified in the April–June 2002 period, the average maturity of the sovereign's domestic debt fell from about 36 months in April to 32 months in September. Also, there was a sharp drop in the stock of domestic government debt toward the end of the year (Table 6), due to the substitution of external and central bank debt for domestic treasury debt. With the successful political transition in early 2003, the average maturity of the debt has started to recover somewhat.

In contrast to Brazil, Chile has experienced a long period of government surpluses and has focused on building an external yield curve to serve as a benchmark for private issuance. Following what the authorities saw as an inadequate assessment of the fundamentals underlying Chilean corporate debt in the aftermath of the Asian crisis, they came to the view that the existence of sovereign external debt instruments would increase foreign investors' research on the country's fundamentals and would contribute to a more accurate pricing of corporate instruments in international markets. Also, the Chilean central bank has built a local yield curve in *Unidades de Fomento* (or UFs, a unit of account linked to the evolution of the CPI), and is currently trying to increase the issuance of peso-denominated debt. This process of nominalization of the central bank debt, aimed at improving the conduct of monetary policy since August 2001, has generated a number of transitional issues as investors get used to the change in numeraire. In particular, the change has disrupted the swap market and the pricing of long-term UF instruments with remaining maturities of less than one year. The authorities have stopped the issuance of UF-denominated debt of less than 360 days, and have successfully issued peso-denominated bonds up to five-year maturities. They hope to gradually continue to extend the peso curve, with the aim of having a coexistence of peso and UF instruments between two and five years, leaving the UF to continue to dominate the long end of the curve.

The main driver behind the growth of the local debt market in Mexico continues to be the federal government, which has financed moderate deficits exclusively in the domestic market since 1996. In the aftermath of the 1994–95 financial crisis, the authorities increased the average life of the stock of domestic debt from eight months in 1995 to 27 months in 2002, in part through the issuance of floating-rate bonds and inflation-indexed bonds. More recently, sustained macroeconomic stability and a low level of local government debt (at just over 12 percent of GDP in 2002; Table 6) has allowed the sovereign to increase substantially the issuance of fixed-rate peso-denominated debt. Issuance of three- and five-year instruments since the first half of 2000 and of 10-year instruments since

July 2001 has allowed the sovereign to bring the share of fixed-rate debt to 26 percent of the total by the end of 2002. The authorities have also taken a number of steps to increase the liquidity of these benchmark instruments, by reopening existing issues and reducing the frequency of auctions. This has, in turn, contributed to a healthy growth of the corporate bond market in 2002–03.

Improving Market Infrastructure

A number of countries have improved their trading and clearing and settlement systems. In particular, the HKMA has recently focused on bringing an international dimension to this aspect of the local bond market. Following the buildup of a paperless clearing, settlement, and custodian system by the Central Money Markets Unit (CMU), and the introduction of a Real Time Gross Settlement (RTGS) payment system and a delivery-versus-payment system for securities in the mid-1990s, the HKMA linked up with Euroclear and Clearstream, as well as with other local markets—including Korea in 1999 and China in 2002. And more recently, it replicated the Hong Kong dollar infrastructure for the U.S. dollar, though use of the facility has so far been moderate.

Many countries have also created a system of primary dealers, but some have not done it or do not even consider it necessary for the adequate functioning of the market. In Chile, for instance, bonds issued by the central bank are placed directly through a public auction in which banks and institutional investors can participate. As they have provided a stable source of demand for the securities, the authorities have not found it necessary to create a system of primary dealers (see Cifuentes, Desormeaux, and Gonzalez, 2002). However, the risks associated with the lack of primary dealers, in terms of undesirable pressures around key auction dates, were exemplified with Poland's experience in early February 2002. According to market participants, the announcement by the Monetary Policy Committee that it intended to stop reducing interest rates (rates had been cut by more than 900 basis points in the previous 12 months), combined with the prospect of a sharp increase in bond issuance (to settle indebtedness problems with the pension funds) and a relative heavy amortization schedule, led a large number of foreign investors to close their positions in the five-year bonds; domestic investors then reportedly rapidly joined in the sale of five-year bonds. Traders in London argued that the lack of primary dealers made it difficult for the Polish authorities to gauge market sentiment in critical junctures. The authorities have been working on a primary dealer system but are rather skeptical as to how much better channels of communication with market participants would help in the management of key auctions.

Developing a Local Investor Base

In Asia, banks continue to be large players in local bond markets. Banks typically hold a large share of short-term government debt to meet liquidity requirements and they dominate the short end of the bond market. However, bond market issuance has recently outpaced the growth of banking sector liabilities in most Asian markets, reflecting an expansion and broadening of the investor base. Long-term institutional investors, such as life insurance companies, have attempted to increase the duration of their assets, and this has made them ready purchasers of longer maturity government securities. However, the asset needs of insurers are unlikely to be met only through government securities, as the yield on such instruments is insufficient to meet the guaranteed returns offered on life insurance products. Hence, in the current low rate environment, insurance companies have been forced to look for a yield pickup in corporate bonds or credit derivatives or to seek gains through more active trading.

The development of a local institutional investor base, as a result of pension system and capital market reforms, also contributes to the increasing depth and stability of local bond markets—especially in the CE-3 and Latin American bond markets. Pension funds hold around 10 percent of total government debt in Hungary, and a somewhat lower percentage in Poland; but they are a steadily growing and stable source of demand. In Latin America, where pension reform started even earlier than in central Europe, pension funds are major players in local bond markets. In Mexico, for instance, private pension funds hold one-fourth of local government bonds, and the percentage is even larger in Chile—where assets under management are 55 percent of GDP (see Roldos, 2003).

Several emerging market countries have also developed a thriving domestic mutual fund industry. For instance, the mutual fund industry in Brazil has more than $150 billion (30 percent of GDP) in assets under management and is the largest holder of government securities together with the banking industry. The number of local mutual funds and their total funds under management has also increased rapidly in Thailand, where they have become important investors in the government bond market. The authorities have made interest income and capital gains from local-bond mutual funds tax exempt, and this has led to the development of more than 80 fixed-income mutual funds with total net asset value of $1.8 billion.

Retail investor demand for bonds has also grown in Asia, through, among other ways, direct sales of bonds through bank branches. In Thailand, retail investors have bought a large share of government bonds to take advantage of the yield pickup relative to bank deposits. Similarly the People's Bank of China has just approved new rules to allow commercial banks to offer sales of interbank-traded government bonds to meet an increased demand from retail investors. Generally, government bonds have paid slightly higher coupons than the one-year savings deposit rates mandated by the central bank.

Foreign participation in local government bond markets has declined markedly since the Russian crisis of 1998, and, despite government efforts to develop bond markets and the removal of capital and exchange controls, foreign participation seems to be meaningful only in the CE-3 countries. The foreign investor base for local bonds in Hungary and Poland is relatively large, as "convergence plays," which take advantage of the declining path of interest rates driven by the expected convergence of inflation rates to euro zone rates, continue to attract substantial foreign interest. Foreigners hold around 12 to 15 percent of total outstanding debt in both markets, but participants estimate that the percentage is closer to 30 to 40 percent when measured relative to total marketable debt or in terms of turnover. In Korea and Mexico, foreign holdings of local debt are around 2 to 3 percent of total outstanding stocks, but here also the figures appear to be an underestimate. Market participants attribute the even lower foreign participation in Brazilian and Chilean local securities markets to a number of factors. Despite the removal of most capital controls and the simplification of investment regulations, the existence of withholding taxes, the possibility of discretionary increases in other taxes—such as the Financial Operations Tax—and the use of indexation and non-standard pricing conventions deter foreigners from buying Brazilian local securities. Foreign investors have had limited interest in local Chilean bonds because of historically low interest rates and the widespread use of UF-denominated instruments.

Corporate Bond Markets

The authorities' efforts to develop local bond markets, combined with the corporate sector efforts to diversify away from refinancing and foreign exchange risks, have contributed to an expansion also of local corporate bond markets in most emerging markets—with the exception perhaps of countries

CHAPTER II EMERGING LOCAL BOND MARKETS

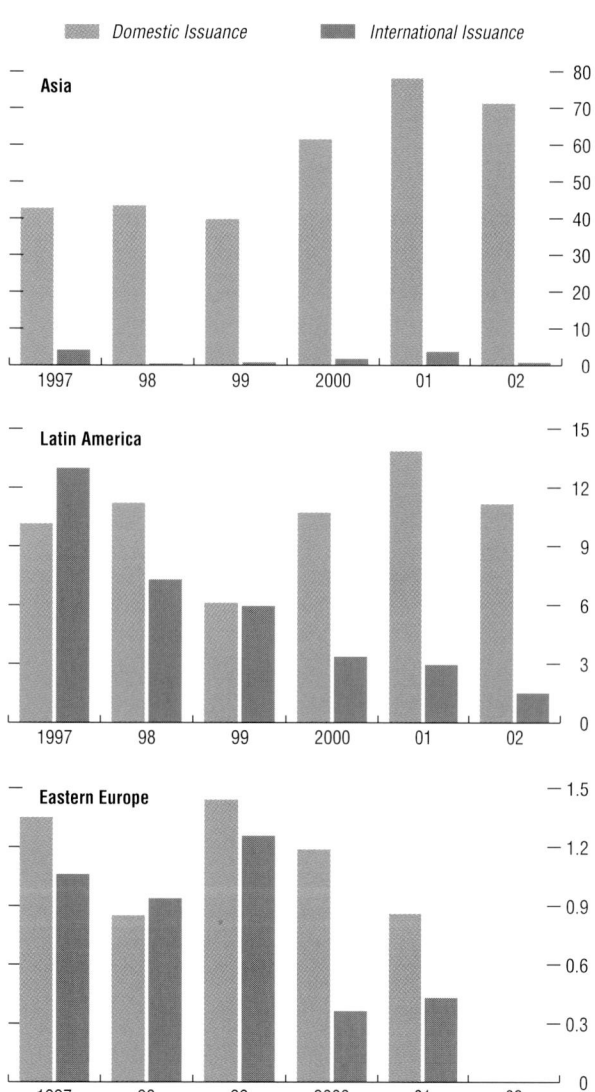

Figure 2. Corporate Bond Issuance in Selected Emerging Markets
(In billions of U.S. dollars)

Sources: IMF staff estimates based on data from local central banks and securities commissions, as well as Capital Net and Bondware.
Notes: Eastern Europe includes Czech Republic and Hungary; Latin America includes Argentina, Brazil, Chile, and Mexico; Asia includes Korea, Malaysia, and Thailand.

in central Europe. Despite this growth, access to local bond issuance has been restricted to top-tier corporates, and it is unclear whether the resilience and size of most of the markets are large enough to consider these markets a meaningful alternative source of funding. Also, in most cases increased local bond issuance has been a result of a favorable interest rate environment, which may be reversed if interest rates rise again.

Since 1997, corporate issuance of local bonds has far exceeded issuance on international markets (see Figure 2). Both Korea and Malaysia already had large corporate bond markets before the crises (11 and 21 percent of GDP in 1997, respectively; Table 6).[44] The dearth of bank financing, as well as the need to restructure balance sheets, gave an additional impetus to these markets, and they more than doubled in size over the past five years. The Korean authorities supported the market through periods of rapid growth and instability after the 1997–98 crisis (see below), as the market struggled to develop a true corporate credit culture. Malaysia's Securities Commission introduced a series of measures to streamline the capital-raising process, which, combined with the process of corporate restructuring, has supported further growth of an already deep corporate bond market. The cost of bond issuance has reportedly fallen below that of bank loans in Malaysia, and bond issuance has dominated bank lending as a source of funding since 1997 (see Moody's, 2002).

Hong Kong SAR and Singapore have encouraged statutory boards (quasi-government entities) and government-linked corporations to issue local currency bonds, but corporate bond issuance remains a small fraction of the market and is concentrated in high-quality issuers. Some foreign corporates have issued in Singapore after the country

---

[44]As most Korean corporated bonds were guaranteed by banks, some analysts considered the bond market to be an extension of the banking system.

opened its market to foreign issuers in August 1998, and foreign banks regularly issue large amounts in the Hong Kong dollar market—usually swapping out the proceeds to foreign currency. However, the volume of issuance by local corporates is still under 10 percent of the total, maturities remain around the five-year mark, and issuers rated lower than single A are rare.

Local corporate bond issuance has also increased in most Latin American countries, and has dominated international bond issuance since 1998 (see Figure 2). Latin corporates have increasingly looked at local markets to refinance external debts and reduce the cost of foreign exchange volatility (see Box 3). However, while Figure 2 shows a clear and growing substitution between domestic and external funding, the total amounts are still rather small—especially when compared with the size of local bond markets in Asia. Domestic corporate bond issuance is less than 1.5 percent of GDP in the major Latin America countries, with the exception of Chile (where issuance reached 4.6 percent of GDP in 2001), compared with 10 to 15 percent of GDP in Korea and Malaysia.

The corporate bond markets in Poland and Hungary are underdeveloped, in part due to the ability of the largest corporates to issue in the Eurobond market or fund themselves through their more highly rated foreign parents. In contrast, and despite a very recent development of the government bond markets, the Czech Republic has a more developed corporate bond market; still, most bonds are small and relatively illiquid (Euroweek, 2001). The Polish corporate bond market is dominated by short-term commercial paper that is distributed on the basis of private placements and has grown rapidly as a result of the fact that commercial paper is exempted from reserve requirements. The Hungarian corporate bond market has also struggled to take off for years, held up by abundant bank credit and some spectacular corporate defaults in the mid-1990s, but analysts are optimistic about the prospects for two reasons. First, several corporates have reached their credit limits with the banks and need an alternative source of finance. Second, the euro-forint market developed quickly in the second quarter of 2001, and this could widen the investor base for local bonds. Finally, the local corporate bond market has grown very rapidly in Russia since 2002, despite the lack of a well-developed government benchmark (see Box 4).

The development of local corporate bond markets is constrained by a variety of factors (see, for instance, Schinasi and Smith, 1998). Market participants highlight the lack of liquidity in secondary markets and of a meaningful investor base with developed credit assessment skills, as well as high costs of local issuance.

Low liquidity in secondary markets reflects such factors as the scale of local issuance, the characteristics of the instruments, and the nature of the investor base. In most emerging markets, only a few large corporates are able to issue bonds on sufficient scale that they create a market where investors can change their trading positions without moving the price against them. In addition, local instruments are not always transparent and hence are difficult to price. In Thailand, for instance, some bonds have complicated structures that may, say, switch from floating interest rates to fixed rates halfway through their term. In Brazil, long-term debentures are usually subject to *repactuacion* clauses that allow for a renegotiation of the terms and conditions of the securities every year. The authorities are working with representatives of the private sector to agree on standard documentation for their bonds that would make them more homogeneous and improve their tradability.[45]

---

[45]Some market participants disagree with the standardization of contracts, as they may constrain the issuers' ability to accommodate company-specific financing needs.

Box 3. External Refinancing Risk in Latin America

The corporate sector in Latin America faced a heavier debt amortization schedule than the sovereign sector in 2002, and the same happened in 2003. As corporates usually take longer to recover access to international capital markets than sovereign borrowers, refinancing risks may be higher for the corporate sector under the current conditions in international markets. The increase in debt amortizations in the corporate sector, from $15 billion in 2001 to $18 billion in 2002 (see Table), is mostly due to an increase in $2.5 billion in the bond segment. In 2003, private sector amortization doubled that of the sovereign and public sectors.

A large fraction of the $4.8 billion of private sector bond amortizations in the second half of 2002 is accounted for by issues from Brazilian corporates and banks, and this contributed to the pressures in the foreign exchange market. However, Chile and Mexico concentrate the larger share of amortization of syndicated loans.

In this context, corporates have switched to local bond markets that have provided a cheaper avenue to refinance external debts coming due, especially in Brazil and Mexico.

Local corporate bond issuance in Mexico reached $3.3 billion in 2002 compared to $2 billion of private sector external bonds coming due in the year, as corporates took advantage of low domestic interest rates (see the Figures). Similarly, Brazilian corporates issued $3.2 billion of local corporate bonds, while the sector faced $4.8 billion in amortizations. Issuance of local bonds was down in Chile in 2002, but the decline was due to the fact that most large corporates took care of their refinancing needs the previous year.

Latin America: External Bond and Loan Amortizations
(In billions of U.S. dollars)

	2001	2002:H1	2002:H2	2002	2003:H1	2003:H2	2003
Bond Amortization	22.6	10.0	10.5	20.5	8.6	12.0	20.6
Private	7.0	4.7	4.8	9.5	2.7	5.3	8.0
Banks	3.6	1.2	2.0	3.2	0.4	1.4	1.8
Corporates	3.5	3.5	2.8	6.3	2.3	3.9	6.2
Public	3.2	1.7	1.0	2.8	1.0	1.4	2.4
Banks	1.6	1.0	0.7	1.7	0.7	0.2	0.9
Nonbanks	1.6	0.7	0.3	1.0	0.3	1.2	1.5
Sovereign	12.4	3.6	4.6	8.2	4.9	5.3	10.2
Loan Amortization	19.5	7.1	8.7	15.8	6.5	18.6	25.1
Private	13.1	5.6	7.3	12.9	5.2	17.1	22.3
Banks	1.1	0.5	1.0	1.5	0.1	6.6	6.7
Corporates	11.9	5.1	6.3	11.4	5.1	10.5	15.6
Public	3.8	1.4	1.5	2.9	1.3	1.4	2.7
Banks	0.2	0.0	0.1	0.2	0.0	0.3	0.3
Nonbanks	3.6	1.4	1.3	2.7	1.3	1.2	2.5
Sovereign	2.6	0.0	0.0	0.0	0.0	0.0	0.0
Total Amortization	42.1	17.0	19.2	36.3	15.0	30.6	45.6
Private	20.1	10.3	12.1	22.4	7.9	22.4	30.3
Banks	4.7	1.7	3.0	4.7	0.5	8.0	8.5
Corporates	15.4	8.6	9.1	17.7	7.4	14.4	21.8
Public	7.0	3.2	2.5	5.7	2.2	2.9	5.1
Banks	1.8	1.1	0.8	1.9	0.7	0.5	1.1
Nonbanks	5.2	2.1	1.7	3.8	1.6	2.4	4.0
Sovereign	15.0	3.6	4.6	8.2	4.9	5.4	10.2

Sources: Capital Data; and IMF staff estimates.

LOCAL BOND MARKETS AS AN ALTERNATIVE SOURCE OF FUNDING

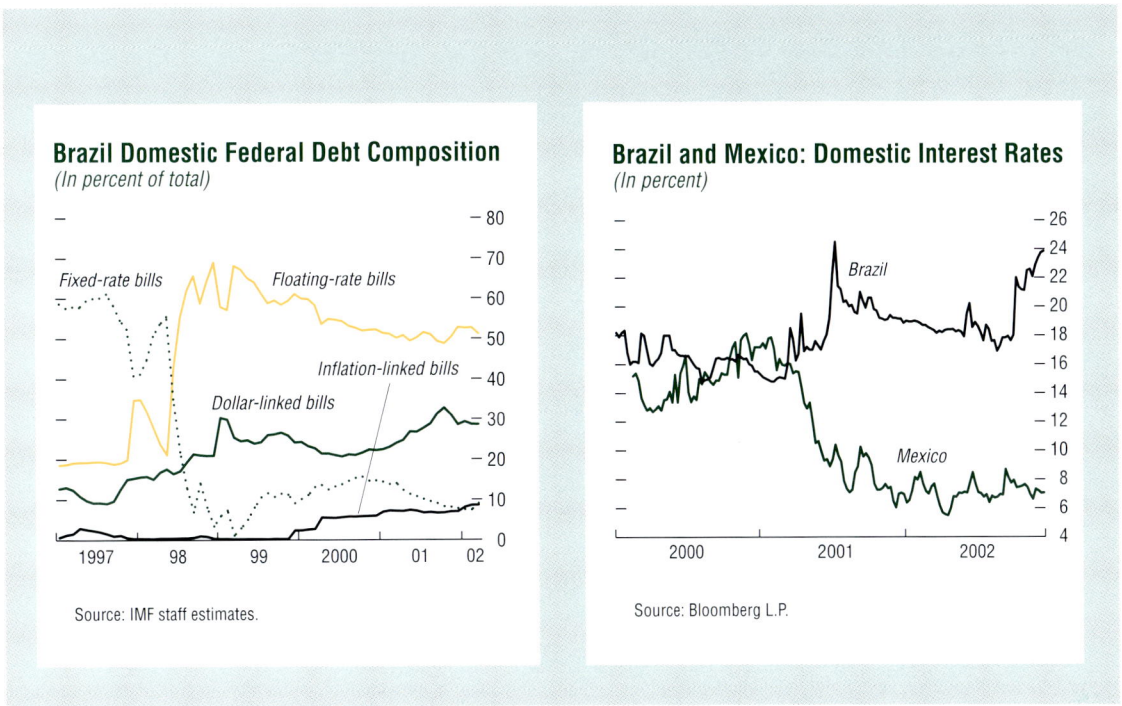

Although the cost of local issuance is in general lower than in international markets, regulatory and other factors have at times made it prohibitively costly to issue in the local market. For example, local investment banks estimate that the cost of placing debt in Chile's local market is one-seventh of that paid for a placement in international markets (see Cifuentes, Desormeaux, and Gutierrez, 2002). The lower relative costs are attributed in part to the small size of Chilean issues (which makes it harder to absorb the large fixed cost of international issuance), to the fact that the local market is open all year round and is not restricted to the "windows of opportunity" provided by international markets, and to the continuously growing appetite of local institutional investors. In contrast, market participants note that bringing an issuer to market in Brazil is relatively expensive. The costs of local issuance, which include those associated with fiduciary agents, lawyers, registration, rating agencies, and bank fees, make it prohibitively expensive to issue debentures in amounts lower than 50 million reais ($20 million). The high costs are partly due to regulations that extend the underwriting process to 60 days, of which the Securities Commission authorization accounts for 30 days and requires that the price be established prior to the authorization request. Similarly, the cost of public issuance in Hong Kong SAR is estimated to be four times that of a private placement. A number of regulatory and cost obstacles make private placements the only profitable way to issue corporate bonds in Poland. For example, analysts noted that a prospectus has to be issued for each issue—ruling out medium-term notes programs—and that prospective issuers must wait a long time for the approval of the Polish Securities and Exchange Commission and must pay high fees to the National Depository of Securities.

The structure of the financial industry may also limit the growth of the local corporate bond market. Analysts note that the CE-3 countries have little intermediary capacity to underwrite corporate bonds, as the large,

Box 4. Local Corporate Bond Market in Russia

In 2002, the ruble-denominated corporate bond market in Russia was the fastest growing local corporate bond market in the emerging markets universe. The total value of all outstanding bonds (excluding the nonmarket issues) more than doubled, increasing from Rb25 billion ($0.8 billion) as of end-2001 to Rb63 billion ($2 billion) as of end-2002. This surge in corporate bond issuance was due to a combination of factors, including the favorable interest rate environment, both globally and domestically; high ruble liquidity on the back of strong petrodollar inflows; and the dearth of bank financing. In contrast with the previous year, the majority of corporate issuers in 2002 were medium and small-size firms from nonresource sectors. As a result, the industry structure of the ruble bond market became more diverse than that of the Russian corporate eurobond market, with oil and gas companies accounting for only about 40 percent of the total market capitalization. In contrast, the much larger corporate eurobond market, with the total value of all outstanding bonds at around $7 billion, is represented mainly by the top-tier companies from the oil and gas sector.

The 1998 crisis provided an impetus for the development of the local corporate bond market by significantly weakening the domestic banking system and shutting off Russian companies from external financing sources. During 1999–2000, the 'veksel' market was the only other form of financing available to local companies besides their accrued earnings. A 'veksel' is similar to commercial paper but, unlike a standard commercial paper, its legal status is not well-defined and, unlike a corporate bond, it does not have to be registered with the Securities Commission. As of mid-2002, the capitalization of the veksel market reportedly stood at around $10 billion, significantly exceeding that of the corporate bond market. On the other hand, Russian banks remained small and undercapitalized and often lacking expertise to lend to companies directly. The main problem faced by banks in Russia is the lack of long-term funding. Since most Russians still prefer to keep their savings in dollars and "under the mattress," most ruble deposits are short-term corporate deposits, rather than longer-term retail money. Also, unlike bonds, bank loans often require posting a collateral and are on average 2 to 3 percentage points more expensive than bonds. As a result, Russian companies prefer bonds to bank loans and similarly, most local banks prefer to have exposure to corporate credit risk via tradable securities rather than loans. Separately, the small size of the local government bond market (less than 5 percent of GDP) and the low level of borrowing by the sovereign created room for a rapid expansion of the corporate bond market (in contrast to the "crowding out" phenomenon in Poland and Hungary).

However, the collapse of the GKO/OFZ market following the 1998 sovereign default left local corporates without a meaningful local currency denominated benchmark. Many floating-rate corporate bonds issued in 2000–01 had their coupon rates tied either to some GKO/OFZ portfolio or to the central bank's refinancing rate or to a liquid sub-sovereign or corporate bond rate. However, high volatility and unpredictability of reference rates eventually forced issuers to switch to fixed-rate bonds. Thus, in the second half of 2002, a three-year bond with a fixed-rate semiannual coupon and embedded put options at 12-month intervals became the most widely used instrument.

The Russian corporate bond market is gradually becoming more mature, with issue sizes increasing, tenors lengthening, and put options being used less frequently. According to local sources, the average "investment period" of the ruble corporate bonds increased from 123 days as of end-2001 to 440 days at end-2002, where "investment period" is defined as the time to the first put option expiration date or to maturity, depending on

Note: This box was prepared by Anna Ilyina.

which yield (yield-to-put option expiration or yield-to-maturity) is the highest. In contrast, the longest-dated Russian corporate eurobond is currently the one issued by Gazprom in February 2003, which matures in March 2013. At the same time, the average yield on a ruble corporate bond with the investment period of one year fell from 21.1 percent as of end-2001 to 15.8 percent as of end-2002, on the back of a continued decline in government bond yields and also partly due to a relative shortage of corporate paper, compared to the abundant banking sector liquidity.

However, along with positive developments, the Russian corporate bond market continues to experience "growing pains" stemming from regulatory inefficiencies and a weak credit information infrastructure similar to that encountered in many other emerging market countries. For example, the existence of a 0.8 percent bond registration fee is reportedly the main reason for a widespread use of bonds with put options and variable-rate coupons, where the coupon rate is determined unilaterally by the issuer and announced shortly before the put option expiration date. These instruments, which appear to be similar to the Brazilian long-term debentures with *repactuacion* clauses, are nontransparent and difficult to price. According to analysts, the proposed reduction of the bond registration fee to 0.2 percent would reduce incentives for Russian companies to use these instruments and could also help accelerate the conversion of the "veksel" market into the corporate bond market. Weak "credit culture" is another problem. S&P and Moody's recently introduced a national scale of credit ratings for Russian companies, but so far awarded such ratings to only a handful of issuers, and the correspondence between ratings and corporate bond spreads remains weak. Meanwhile, the rapid expansion of the market led to a perceived deterioration of the average credit quality of corporate issuers, with more medium and small-size companies tapping the market in 2002 compared to 2001. Some market participants believe that a deterioration in the pool of issuers, combined with the continued decline in spreads, suggests that pricing may not be entirely efficient and that the credit risk assessment capabilities of investors may have to be strengthened.

The investor base for ruble corporate bonds is not sufficiently diverse and remains heavily dominated by local banks. According to local market sources, its current structure is as follows: 45 to 50 percent, Moscow based banks (most of which are also the underwriters); 20 to 25 percent, regional banks; 20 percent, insurance companies and nongovernment pension funds; and 10 percent, other (including about 3 percent, retail investors). The top 20 banks are also the main liquidity providers in the secondary bond market, deriving part of their trading income from buying/selling corporate bonds, while most of the medium and smaller-size banks typically hold bonds to maturity. Regional banks that have relatively expensive liabilities typically seek higher-yielding paper. Foreign investors can invest in ruble denominated corporate bonds using N-accounts (rubles are not freely convertible into foreign exchange) and K-accounts (rubles are freely convertible into the foreign exchange for coupon payments). Although until recently foreign investors remained on the sidelines, their participation in some recent primary placements was notable. Asset management companies that invest on behalf of mutual funds are currently not allowed to participate in primary bond placements because the mutual fund regulations explicitly prohibit their managers from investing in securities that do not have a history of quotes. Some buy-side market participants note that a relaxation of this restriction would significantly increase their interest in the domestic corporate bond market.

foreign-owned banks have little incentive to devote capital to such activity in the local market, and the local banks and brokerages typically lack the resources to do it. Also, banks in Thailand appeared reluctant to underwrite bond issuance because they feared competition from the bond market, while banks in Hong Kong SAR, eager to take advantage of the fees involved in the process, have begun to underwrite bonds. In Brazil, "firm underwriting" procedures are used by the local banks as a tool to compete with the foreign banks.[46] According to international investment banks operating in Brazil, local banks' willingness to adopt the more expensive underwriting procedure is partly explained by their appetite for credit risk, different risk management strategies compared with foreign-owned institutions, and the not-so-solid "Chinese walls" between their investment bank and asset management arms, which allow them to place some of the issuance with the pension and mutual funds under their control.

The lack of a stable and large institutional investor base, and/or restrictions on their asset holdings, is also seen as a major constraint on market development. Although some countries in Asia have started to develop privately managed pension funds, it takes time for these institutions to accumulate the funds and to have an impact in the market (see IMF, 2001; and Moody's, 2001). In Malaysia, life insurance companies are important players in fixed-income markets, but they cannot invest more than 15 percent of their portfolio in unsecured bonds and loans, and they can only invest in highly rated corporate bonds. Similarly, restrictions on the use of derivatives in the CE-3 and Latin American countries' pension funds have limited the funds' appetite for fixed-income products, as they cannot hedge interest rate risks.

Some market participants note that most emerging local bond markets lack sophistication in credit risk assessments and that the full development of a credit culture is still some way off. For instance, they note that many investors in Asia treat quasi-government issues almost on an equal footing with the sovereign and that they price local issues on the basis of name recognition, without a deeper analysis of credit fundamentals. However, the degree of sophistication in the pricing of corporate bonds is relatively high in Chile, and it is gradually improving in Brazil. Local rating agencies have achieved a relatively high degree of professionalism in Chile, reflecting more than 20 years of experience in the market and the important presence of the major international rating agencies. In Brazil, market participants complain that there is not enough price discrimination and that the mutual funds buy the bonds by name recognition, without pricing adequately company fundamentals or the existence of guarantees or other enhancements. Nevertheless, participants see the fact that most issuers are obtaining two ratings—rather than only one, as required by the regulations—as a sign that the market is gradually maturing.

Korea's experience provides an interesting illustration of the potential role of the corporate bond market as an alternative source of funding, as well as of the problems that may arise when guarantees distort price discovery. As the supply of bank credit dried up in the aftermath of the financial crisis of 1997–98, bond issuance increased substantially, operating to some degree as an alternative source of funding. However, issuance was concentrated in the Big Five chaebol, which were also owners of the largest investment trust companies (ITCs), the main investors in corporate bonds. The collapse of the third largest chaebol led to a run on the ITCs and the associ-

---

[46]Firm underwriting is an arrangement whereby investment banks make outright purchases from the issuer of the securities and they sell them at a profit or loss depending on market conditions; under alternative arrangements, bankers agree to do their best effort to sell an issue to the public, but they could cancel part of the sales and forgo the fees.

ated sell-off in the bond market forced the authorities to restrict redemptions and provide liquidity support to the bond market. Moreover, the surge of bond financing in 1998 led to a wave of refinancing in 2000–2001 that, combined with the removal of guarantees and the introduction of mark-to-market in the ITCs, prompted further governmental support of the market through the creation of a bond stabilization fund and official guarantees. A key support measure expired at the end of 2001 as planned, and the authorities are phasing out other support for the corporate bond market over time.

Finally, in several emerging markets the major obstacle to the growth of corporate bond markets is the crowding out by government bond issuance. In Brazil, for instance, government securities offer domestic investors low credit risk, ample secondary market liquidity, high yields, and—in many cases—protection against exchange rate, inflation, and interest rate risks through indexed bonds. Hence, only strong local corporates willing to pay rates in excess of 20 percent on three-year bonds are able to bid for domestic investors' money given the formidable competition posed by the government. These issuers are concentrated in highly rated companies from the telecommunications, utilities, and natural resources industries. In many cases, corporate bonds had to be enhanced with guarantees to become attractive enough to investors. Similarly, the abundant supply of government paper in the CE-3 countries also crowds out private issuance. The inverted yield curve in Hungary and Poland is also a hindrance to corporate bond demand, as investors who can get 10 percent risk-free returns on government paper have little incentive to seek out credit yield pickup in medium-term corporate bonds.

Secondary Markets and the Role of Foreign Investors

The increasing importance of local bond markets can also be seen in the evolution of secondary market activity, as measured by trading volumes. According to EMTA's debt trading volume survey, local market volumes reached almost half of total debt volumes in 2002,[47] followed by 35 percent in Eurobonds and 15 percent in Brady bonds (see Table 7). While trading volume in external debt instruments fell in 2002 to less than half its 1997 level, trading volume in domestic instruments held up and has recovered to its pre-Asian crisis level. The overall declining trend, as well as the high regional and country variation, is mostly due to the string of crises and to the role played by foreign investors, who are considered critical to the market's liquidity and direction (see, for instance, Deutsche Bank, 2000). Analysts note, however, that governments' efforts to develop the markets have focused more on the primary market than on the transparency and efficiency of the secondary markets; and that transaction taxes, as well as underdeveloped repurchase (repo) and derivatives markets, limit secondary market activities.

The Asian crisis brought that region's trading volumes in local instruments to one-third of the pre-crisis levels, but they have recovered to more than twice their 1996 level, outstripping the increase in stocks outstanding. Trading volumes have grown sharply in Korea, with the introduction of mark-to-market regulations, a system of over-the-counter inter-dealer brokers, increased foreign participation, and availability of hedging instruments—in particular, the rapid growth in the three-year Korean treasury bond futures contract.[48] Similarly, secondary market

---

[47]In the last quarter of 2002 volumes in local instruments surpassed those in external instruments for the first time since the survey was conducted.

[48]Emerging Markets Trade Association (EMTA) data have the advantage of a common methodology across countries, but the fact that a large fraction of reporting firms are international banks means that sometimes individual country data differ from local sources. In particular, the latter show continued growth in trading volumes in Korea and Thailand, in contrast to Table 7.

CHAPTER II EMERGING LOCAL BOND MARKETS

Table 7. Emerging Market Debt Trading Volume Survey
(In millions of U.S. dollars)

	1995	1996	1997	1998	1999	2000	2001	2002
Overall	2,738,815	5,296,931	5,915,995	4,173,881	2,184,839	2,846,503	3,483,950	3,068,377
Local instruments	571,141	1,187,899	1,505,996	1,176,371	598,707	992,982	1,516,565	1,411,436
External instruments	1,813,354	3,344,130	3,737,317	2,561,498	1,397,688	1,648,770	1,828,487	1,522,056
Asia[1]	3,832	99,228	64,963	118,997	83,441	229,424	252,719	325,729
Local instruments	1,947	72,966	48,415	42,303	24,110	165,779	168,022	249,242
External instruments	320	14,724	15,162	69,337	55,770	60,994	79,819	71,214
China	80	436	1,807	9,695	4,663	2,656	6,354	3,192
Local instruments	6	73	39	6,128	0	108	942	272
External instruments	74	355	1,650	3,441	4,072	2,206	4,898	2,483
Hong Kong SAR		40,909	45,760	37,377	16,453	98,283	86,955	119,620
Local instruments		30,120	42,919	29,907	9,925	91,393	69,979	101,963
External instruments		6,824	2,840	7,447	4,896	5,648	13,915	13,812
India	924	9,317	3,065	3,017	6,842	15,864	15,802	25,266
Local instruments	3	2,824	541	1,613	4,973	13,159	12,134	24,016
External instruments		6,155	2,377	1,289	1,843	2,696	3,658	1,186
Korea	57	411	6,045	60,925	38,088	50,903	44,146	76,722
Local instruments		280	737	2,952	5,803	22,173	17,936	59,247
External instruments	54	127	5,293	50,893	31,336	28,228	25,496	17,211
Malaysia	842	11,548	5,095	4,319	10,880	20,238	30,266	38,522
Local instruments	675	9,567	2,323	650	308	8,867	15,192	18,256
External instruments	143	896	1,690	3,669	10,542	11,084	14,950	20,008
Singapore	237	1,213	223	116	3,040	30,177	63,627	56,140
Local instruments		1,005	66	71	2,668	22,634	48,979	41,440
External instruments	31	0	157	45	373	7,518	14,635	14,700
Thailand	1,692	35,394	2,968	3,548	3,475	11,303	5,569	6,267
Local instruments	1,263	29,097	1,790	982	433	7,445	2,860	4,048
External instruments	18	367	1,155	2,553	2,708	3,614	2,267	1,814
Europe[1]	249,155	495,243	785,045	939,660	314,286	429,424	505,498	470,695
Local instruments	44,537	79,071	274,033	364,977	156,701	149,369	163,048	158,770
External instruments	72,467	185,649	200,234	328,268	117,475	212,918	327,585	296,336
Czech Republic	3,575	14,223	8,656	4,867	3,855	2,274	14,270	7,851
Local instruments	3,235	8,310	4,413	3,310	696	1,372	10,595	5,349
External instruments	341	5,454	3,981	1,534	3,122	888	3,608	2,402
Hungary	824	3,461	3,768	10,405	16,627	14,942	34,419	32,092
Local instruments	202	1,943	1,854	4,972	8,672	5,562	29,013	25,767
External instruments	622	1,518	1,894	4,611	7,930	9,367	4,359	6,324
Poland	96,184	81,055	69,683	94,837	24,554	48,763	90,321	103,200
Local instruments	26,397	9,070	29,190	56,893	9,414	33,083	73,217	76,868
External instruments	43,487	66,227	39,183	37,691	15,114	15,658	17,103	26,288
Russia	144,977	380,499	648,414	684,364	123,349	241,316	299,468	244,642
Local instruments	12,175	51,255	195,519	191,681	19,685	36,373	27,562	27,025
External instruments	26,952	105,129	143,774	250,261	64,337	139,683	259,405	202,967
Turkey	3,595	16,005	54,524	145,187	145,901	122,129	67,020	82,910
Local instruments	2,528	8,493	43,057	108,121	118,234	72,979	22,661	23,761
External instruments	1,065	7,321	11,402	34,171	26,972	47,322	43,110	58,355
Latin America[1]	2,001,533	3,700,816	4,063,864	2,554,276	1,444,579	1,809,150	2,236,773	1,720,887
Local instruments	481,909	830,079	961,695	632,527	381,211	596,058	1,001,412	770,208
External instruments	1,371,164	2,480,513	2,829,672	1,781,350	947,368	1,102,625	1,134,868	858,614
Argentina	609,678	1,292,462	1,235,710	612,390	318,940	365,772	383,760	38,506
Local instruments	98,062	400,215	249,845	111,251	52,911	68,916	39,591	752
External instruments	486,620	804,424	901,243	471,968	254,409	287,608	339,747	37,737

SECONDARY MARKETS AND THE ROLE OF FOREIGN INVESTORS

Table 7 (concluded)

	1995	1996	1997	1998	1999	2000	2001	2002
Brazil	877,412	1,441,454	1,796,444	1,268,856	801,596	768,985	721,035	707,136
Local instruments	173,246	120,539	312,790	156,753	165,367	106,576	82,391	50,630
External instruments	622,937	1,118,531	1,370,858	1,026,460	538,671	579,202	563,092	579,283
Chile	4,308	20,504	51,811	32,549	11,402	12,721	20,896	26,410
Local instruments	368	10,550	45,002	29,747	6,575	8,690	11,038	16,139
External instruments	3,706	8,665	6,610	2,631	4,824	4,002	9,858	10,227
Mexico	510,135	946,396	979,899	640,481	312,641	661,672	1,111,082	948,835
Local instruments	210,233	298,775	354,058	334,776	156,358	411,876	868,392	702,687
External instruments	257,901	548,893	550,961	280,291	149,464	231,813	222,171	231,367
Other[2]	484,295	1,001,644	1,002,123	560,948	342,533	378,505	488,960	551,066
Local instruments	42,748	205,783	221,853	136,564	36,685	81,776	184,083	233,216
External instruments	369,403	663,244	692,249	382,543	277,075	272,233	286,215	295,892

Source: Emerging Markets Trade Association.
[1]Regional totals are based on the countries in this table and, hence, do not include all countries in the region.
[2]All other countries of the survey not in this table.
Notes: External instruments include *Brady Bonds, Non-Brady Bonds,* and *Eurobonds. Loans* and *Debt Options & Warrants* categories of the survey are not included in local instruments or external instruments. However, these categories are in the totals by countries, regions and overall.

activity has increased in Malaysia, despite the existence of capital controls and some structural problems—such as the lack of mark-to-market regulations (see Deutsche Bank, 2001b). Another constraint to the development of secondary market activity is the underdevelopment of repo markets. In Thailand, for instance, all repo transactions are done bilaterally with the Bank of Thailand, as private repo transactions are subject to a gross transactions tax that makes them prohibitively expensive. This tax has also prevented the establishment of a short-term interbank rate that would serve as the basis for the swap market. Foreign participation has remained low, as a result of these structural weaknesses and—more important—because of the low interest rate environment. Reflecting the easing of global monetary conditions and local financial policies, yield curves in most Asian countries shifted down and steepened during 2001 (see Figure 3). Short-term interest rates fell to under the 2 percent level in Hong Kong SAR, Singapore, and Thailand by the end of the year, while longer-term rates were supported in part by active government efforts to extend the duration of bond issues and market participants' expectations of interest rate increases. In 2002 and the first half of 2003, yield curves continued to shift downward and flattened in an almost deflationary environment for the region (see Figure 3).

Despite having one of the largest stock of outstanding domestic government bonds, China's secondary markets are quite illiquid, reflecting the existing segmentation across investors, instruments, and trading mechanisms. There are two separate markets for bond trading: the stock exchange and the interbank market. Since 1997 banks have been banned from the stock exchange and trade solely in the interbank market. Until recently, individual investors were allowed to trade only in the stock exchange, while securities houses and investment funds were allowed to trade in both markets.

The crises in some countries caused a collapse in secondary market activity in European local bond markets, while trading of external instruments recovered to precrisis levels in 2001. For example, nonresident investors were holding about one-third of Russian treasury domestic securities (with a value of around $20 billion) by mid-1998 (see IMF, 1998a), and the losses incurred in the aftermath of the devaluation of the ruble and

Figure 3. Selected Countries Domestic Yield Curves[1]
(In percent)

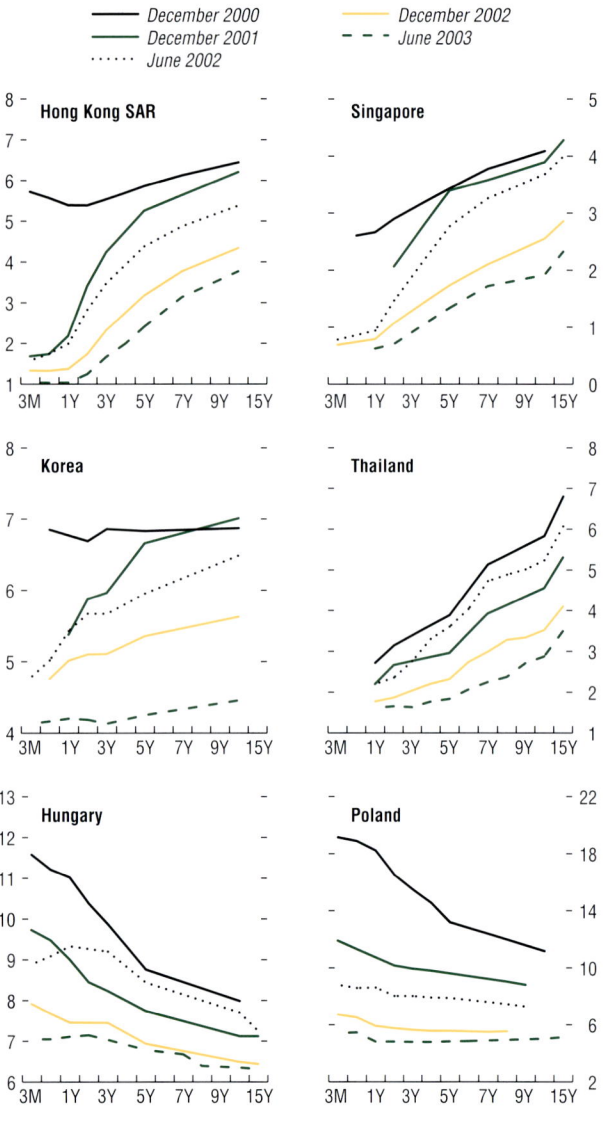

Source: Bloomberg L.P.
[1]June 2003 data are at the beginning of June.

default have meant that they have stayed out of that market—and perhaps out of several other local bond markets. Similarly, foreign holdings of Turkish domestic securities were around 10 to 15 percent by mid-2000 (a percentage similar to that of the Mexican crisis), when pressures in the treasury bill market began, but they have declined markedly after the November 1999 sell-off.

Increased issuance and foreign participation contributed to very rapid growth in secondary market trading in the CE-3 countries. Most foreign investors engaged in "convergence plays" are "real money"—that is, institutional investor funds from western Europe that have a positive long-term view on the region and take unhedged positions in medium-term local currency government bonds in order to capture the gains from declines in local interest rates and exchange rate appreciations that are viewed as likely to occur as these countries near access to the European Union.[49] Although the exposure to the domestic bond markets is not a one-way bet, especially after the widening of the exchange rate band of the Hungarian forint in May 2001 and the recent volatility of the Polish zloty, real money investors have a long-term view and do not seem to worry much about short-term foreign exchange rate fluctuations. Leveraged investors, such as hedge funds and the proprietary trading desks of the major banks, have a much smaller presence that tends to increase in periods of high volatility. Market participants see the large ratio of real to leveraged money as providing stability to the foreign investor base in the CE-3 local debt markets, but the hedging behavior of institutional investors and other features of the investor base have at times been a source of instability. For instance, the ten-

---

[49]Foreign ownership of government securities continued to increase in the second half of 2002 and early 2003—especially after the Irish referendum—reaching almost 40 percent in Hungary and 20 percent in Poland.

dency of investors to dynamically hedge during periods of increased exchange rate volatility has sometimes led to "snowballing effects." This was seen in Poland by mid-2001, when weak local market conditions combined with increased hedging by foreign holders of zloty-denominated bonds to lead to a sell-off in the local foreign exchange market. Also, the sharp flattening and downward shift of local market yield curves in 2002–03 has reduced the attractiveness of convergence plays (Figure 3).[50]

Trading volumes in Latin American local instruments increased 68 percent in 2001, with growth in volumes of Mexican instruments dominating the decline of those from Argentina and Brazil. Trading volumes in all three local markets declined in 2002, following Argentina's default in December 2001. Still, trading in Mexican local instruments accounts for more than half of the local emerging market universe according to the EMTA survey—a reflection of the appeal of Mexican debt for crossover investors, among other factors. This fact gives credence to market participants' view that the role of foreign investors in the Mexican market is larger than that suggested by official estimates of foreign holdings of local bonds.[51] Also, trading volumes in the Mexican local market have increased as a result of the relative increase in fixed-rate bonds,[52] while the opposite has occurred in the Brazilian local markets. Liquidity in the latter market has also been hampered by the bank debit tax (the CPMF).

Conclusion

Emerging local bond markets are gradually but steadily becoming an alternative source of funding for sovereigns and, to a lesser extent, corporate borrowers. To some degree, existing corporate bond markets served as an alternative source of finance in Hong Kong SAR, Korea, and Malaysia after the 1997–98 financial crises. Progress in these and other markets over the last five years has meant that these markets are likely to buffer the impact of future disruptions in other financial markets. The rapid growth of local corporate bond issuance in Latin America is substituting for the reduced access to international capital markets, but mostly for top-tier corporates. Analysts hope that the strong growth in private pension funds, combined with the support of more transparent government benchmarks and better corporate governance and transparency, may extend the benefits of corporate bond markets to lower-tier credits.

Progress in the development of secondary markets is somewhat less satisfactory, and some market participants are concerned that a reversal of the interest rate cycle might lead to excessive adjustments in bond prices, especially in those markets where hedging instruments are unavailable or highly illiquid. Despite improved liquidity, uncertainties on EU accession and large fiscal deficits could still generate periods of market turbulence in the CE-3 countries. Foreign participation continues to be relatively large in these markets and has so far contributed to a deepening of secondary markets. Increased crossover interest in local bonds has been seen only in liquid markets with plain vanilla 5- or 10-year fixed-rate bonds. A large share of indexed securities has kept foreigners away from local Latin bond markets, but things seem to be gradually improving in Chile and Mexico.

---

[50]Further moves toward accession continue to underpin the attractiveness of convergence plays, while loose macroeconomic policies and uncertain exchange rate outlooks undermine them.

[51]This may be, in part, due to the fact that foreign investors take positions in local bond markets through total return swaps, and the actual bond holding is registered with a local bank.

[52]While the daily trading volume of indexed bonds was just 10 billion pesos (with an outstanding stock of 349 billion pesos), the corresponding figure for fixed-rate bonds was 140 billion pesos (for an outstanding stock of 107 billion pesos) in March 2002.

CHAPTER III EMERGING EQUITY MARKETS

Ramana Ramaswamy

One of the key issues in developing local securities markets as a stable source of funding for corporates is the development of an adequate domestic and international investor base. The scale and stability of that investor base will be influenced fundamentally by the nature of the returns and portfolio diversification benefits associated with holding local securities. This chapter therefore analyzes emerging market equities from two perspectives. First, it looks at the performance of this asset class from the perspective of global investors and considers how this performance may affect the scale and volatility of equity-related capital flows. Second, it examines emerging market equities as an alternative source of finance for the corporate sector, and analyzes how equity issuance in emerging markets has fared in relation to bank financing.

Emerging Market Equities as an Asset Class for Foreign Investors

The global investor base for emerging market equities includes dedicated emerging market funds, global or international funds that allocate a portion of their assets to emerging market equities in order to track either a world or regional equity index, and tactical investors, such as hedge funds. While the emerging market allocations of global equity funds are typically small—around 4 percent of total assets—the absolute amounts of these allocations can be sizable in relation to the market capitalization of emerging stock markets; for instance, the emerging market exposure of global equity funds (both dedicated and nondedicated) is estimated to have reached over a $100 billion in 2002 (about half the size of total market capitalization in Korea). For tactical investors in emerging markets, the objective is to achieve high absolute returns through market timing, given the high volatility of this asset class. For global equity funds, emerging market equities could provide a diversification play. Adding emerging market equities to portfolios dominated by mature market equities can at times provide a more favorable risk-return profile than investing exclusively in mature market equities, particularly when returns between the two assets are not closely correlated.

The global investor's perspective on emerging market equities is somewhat different from that of the local investor, in part because the alternative investment opportunities facing the two are often rather different. Despite the strong drive toward financial market liberalization and integration, a number of emerging markets continue to have capital controls, and prudential and regulatory restrictions on the portfolio choices of institutional investors may constrain both local and global investors in different ways. The international investor is typically interested in the foreign currency returns available from investing in emerging market equities, and has access to several other classes of equities as alternatives; dedicated international emerging market funds, in particular, expect to obtain an equity premium on this asset class over longer periods. Local equity investors are mainly interested in local currency returns and risks, and for many of them the assets available for investment are much more restricted than for the global investor. Until recently, for example, retail investors in many emerging markets have had little access to fixed-income instruments; the alternatives in practice have involved the decision of whether to place money in a bank, to buy government bonds, or to invest it in stocks. As local fixed-income instruments become a more viable asset class in emerging markets in the future, the existence of an equity premium that compensates for the additional risk is likely to become an important issue for the investment strategy of local investors.

In any event, the global investor's decision to invest in emerging equities is driven by risk-adjusted returns and by the potential portfolio diversification benefits associated with the extent of the correlation of these returns with the rest of his/her portfolio. In the next sections, the performance of emerging equity markets is reviewed, with a view to inferring how this performance affected the investment behavior of global investors as the asset class matured during the past decade.

Emerging Equity Market Performance

Emerging market equity returns have been relatively poor—both in absolute and relative terms—during the past decade. Between 1990 and 2002, the average annual return on the S&P/IFCI Composite[53] was about 3.9 percent—less than half of the returns available from investing in the S&P 500 index or the NASDAQ. The returns on the Asian component of the IFCI Composite have, in fact, been in borderline negative territory; Latin America accounts for the bulk of the positive returns that this asset class has provided during the decade. In contrast to emerging market equities, emerging market international bonds have provided high returns. Indeed, investors tracking J.P. Morgan's emerging bond index, EMBI+, could have obtained average annual returns of almost 15 percent between 1990 and 2002. Comparison with other "riskier" asset classes provides much the same story—U.S. high-yield instruments generated almost twice the return of emerging market equities in this period.

Not only have returns on emerging market equities been low, but volatility has been high, with Sharpe ratios for emerging market equity returns being significantly lower than those for both the S&P 500 and the EMBI+ (Table 8).[54] The cumulative impact of the underperformance of emerging market equities over the decade is illustrated starkly in Figure 4. One hundred dollars invested in January 1990 in a fund tracking the IFCI Composite would have grown to $166 at the end of 2002. The same investment tracking the S&P 500 index, in contrast, would have grown to $356. Investors tracking the EMBI+, however, would have been rewarded by asset growth of almost six times over the period.

Splitting the last 10 years into the pre- and post-Mexican crisis phases—a benchmark often used to delineate the start of the increasing internationalization of emerging market crises—offers interesting insights. Between 1990 and 1994, the average annual returns on the benchmark emerging market equity index was about 16 percent—twice that of the returns available from tracking the S&P 500, and even somewhat higher than that of EMBI+. The Sharpe ratio for the IFCI Composite was also higher than that for the S&P 500, associated with a relatively lower volatility of returns for emerging market equities in this period. All that changed dramatically during 1995–2002. The returns on the IFCI Composite averaged a negative 3.75 percent, in contrast to about 10 percent returns on the S&P 500 and about 15 percent for EMBI+. Volatility of equity returns also

---

[53]For many global investors, the benchmark used to measure emerging equity markets returns is the S&P/IFCI composite index. It is U.S. dollar based, excludes stocks that foreign investors are restricted from buying in emerging markets, and adjusts for float, liquidity, and market capitalization. An alternative benchmark index for emerging market investors is the MSCI Emerging Market Free (EMF). The main difference between the two indices is that the MSCI EMF attempts to proxy the industry coverage of the local index, while the IFCI composite includes stocks solely on liquidity and accessibility considerations. Both indices are used extensively as benchmarks by emerging market funds and are highly correlated.

[54]The Sharpe ratio equals the difference between the return on an instrument and a risk-free rate of return divided by the standard deviation of the return on the instrument.

CHAPTER III   EMERGING EQUITY MARKETS

Table 8. Equity and Bond Returns

	2001–2002:Q4			1990–1994		
	Returns	Standard deviation	Sharpe ratio	Returns	Standard deviation	Sharpe ratio
S&P/IFCI Composite[1]	−1.13	26.0	−0.23	16.02	20.6	0.42
Asia	4.01	29.5	−0.03	12.35	24.2	0.21
EMEA	1.10	24.4	−0.15	−2.57	35.2	−0.28
Latin America	−12.68	32.2	−0.54	27.40	29.2	0.69
MSCI EAFE[2]	−19.89	19.6	−1.26	0.31	19.4	−0.36
S&P 500	−18.81	20.1	−1.17	8.34	12.4	0.09
NASDAQ	−30.76	38.7	−0.92	10.06	17.6	0.16
EMBI+ Brady Broad[3]	13.65	12.9	0.68	14.43	14.0	0.51
Merrill Lynch U.S. High Yield	2.43	11.1	−0.21	11.32	6.4	0.63

Sources: Bloomberg L.P.; and Datastream.
[1]Asia: China, India, Indonesia, Korea, Malaysia, Pakistan, The Philippines, Sri Lanka, Taiwan, and Thailand. EMEA: Czech Republic, Greece, Hungary, Poland, Russia, Slovakia, Turkey, Egypt, Israel, Jordan, Morocco, South Africa, and Zimbabwe. Latin America: Argentina, Brazil, Chile, Colombia, Mexico, Peru, and Venezuela.
[2]EAFE stands for Europe, Australia, and Far East.
[3]EMBI+ Brady Broad started in 1991.

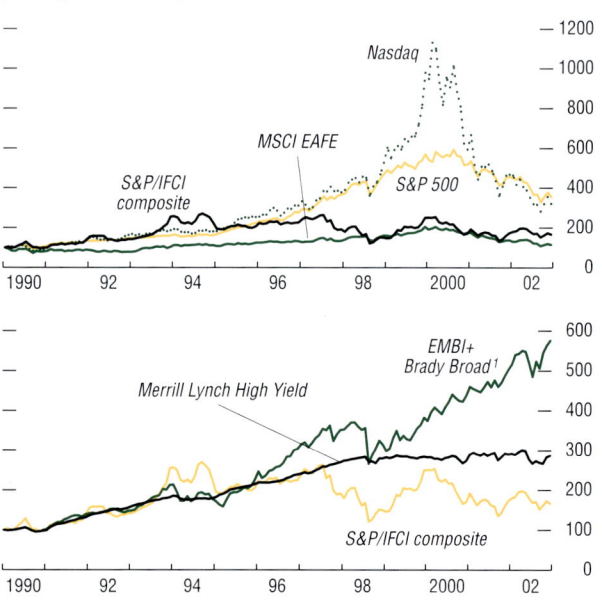

Figure 4. Equity and Bond Performances
(January 1990 = 1000)

Sources: Bloomberg L.P.; and Standard and Poor's.
[1]December 1990 = 100.

increased significantly in emerging markets in the post-Mexican crisis period.

The performance of emerging equity markets during the 1990s stands in sharp contrast to that of mature market equities. On the one hand, for advanced economies, the existence of an ex post equity premium—that is, higher returns available over the long run from holding stocks compared to the yields on a risk-free rate, usually a benchmark treasury bond—is generally accepted as a stylized fact; the premium is perceived as the higher compensation required for holding the riskier asset. The debate on the equity premium has essentially centered on whether it is "rational" for the premium to be as high as the realized 6 to 7 percent for holding stocks rather than bonds. Some have argued that the equity premium in the United States indeed has been historically high, but that the run-up in U.S. stock prices in the latter half of the 1990s, and the accompanying higher valuations and lower implied expected returns, has reduced the equilibrium equity premium, as investors have gradually adapted to the idea of holding stocks as a longer-term asset.[55] In emerging

[55]See, for instance, Clement (2001); and Constantinides, Donaldson, and Mehra (2002).

	1995–2002			1990–2002	
Returns	Standard deviation	Sharpe ratio	Returns	Standard deviation	Sharpe ratio
−3.72	25.6	−0.37	3.87	23.9	−0.10
−9.22	31.4	−0.48	−0.93	28.9	−0.25
3.49	24.4	−0.09	1.16	28.9	−0.18
−1.74	32.0	−0.23	9.47	31.2	0.10
−0.54	16.6	−0.38	−0.21	17.7	−0.37
9.80	17.0	0.24	9.24	15.3	0.19
7.18	32.0	0.04	8.29	27.3	0.07
14.67	17.5	0.51	14.59	16.3	0.51
5.86	6.9	0.02	7.96	6.7	0.24

markets, however, the equity premium has been *negative* over the period 1990–2002—the return on the IFCI Composite being almost 2 percentage points lower on average than that from holding the 10-year U.S. treasury bond.

Portfolio Diversification and Emerging Equity Markets

The negative equity premium on emerging market equities raises the issue of why a global investor ought to have an exposure to this asset class. It also raises concerns about the future viability of this asset class. As noted above, another determinant of foreign investor interest in emerging market stocks is their potential return enhancing and/or risk reducing function in broader equity portfolios. How much of that has materialized?

Figure 5 illustrates the historic risk-return trade-offs available for different portfolio combinations of emerging market and U.S. stocks, with a focus on international investors willing to allocate up to 10 percent of their assets to emerging market equities. During the period from January 1990 to December 2002, a portfolio consisting only of emerging market stocks was ex post inefficient, as it returned the lowest possible annual average return (3.9 percent) for the highest possible risk (23.4 percent). In contrast, a portfolio that included only U.S. stocks would have provided a return of about 9 percent, the highest possible portfolio return. Hence, U.S. stocks were clearly more attractive than emerging market stocks from a tactical perspective—that is, when the focus is exclusively on returns. Moreover, emerging market stocks did not offer much in the way of diversification benefits in this period, as a 10 percent allocation to emerging markets did little to change portfolio risk, while providing a lower annual return of about 8.5 percent. For the investor wanting to minimize risk, the minimum variance portfolio would have consisted of only a 2 percent allocation to emerging market stocks.

In contrast to the experience of the decade as a whole, the first five years of the 1990s proved rewarding for global funds willing to hold emerging market stocks. A portfolio fully allocated to emerging market stocks not only experienced the highest return (about 16 percent annually), but also offered diversification benefits to international investors. A portfolio of exclusively U.S. stocks was ex post inefficient, returning 8.4 percent for a risk of 12.5 percent, whereas a 10 percent allocation to emerging markets would have provided about a 9 percent annual return for a marginal risk reduction. Such an allocation would have also been the minimum variance portfolio. The post-Mexican crisis period has been a troubling one for emerging market equities. Between 1995 and 2002, a portfolio composed exclusively of emerging market stocks would

CHAPTER III EMERGING EQUITY MARKETS

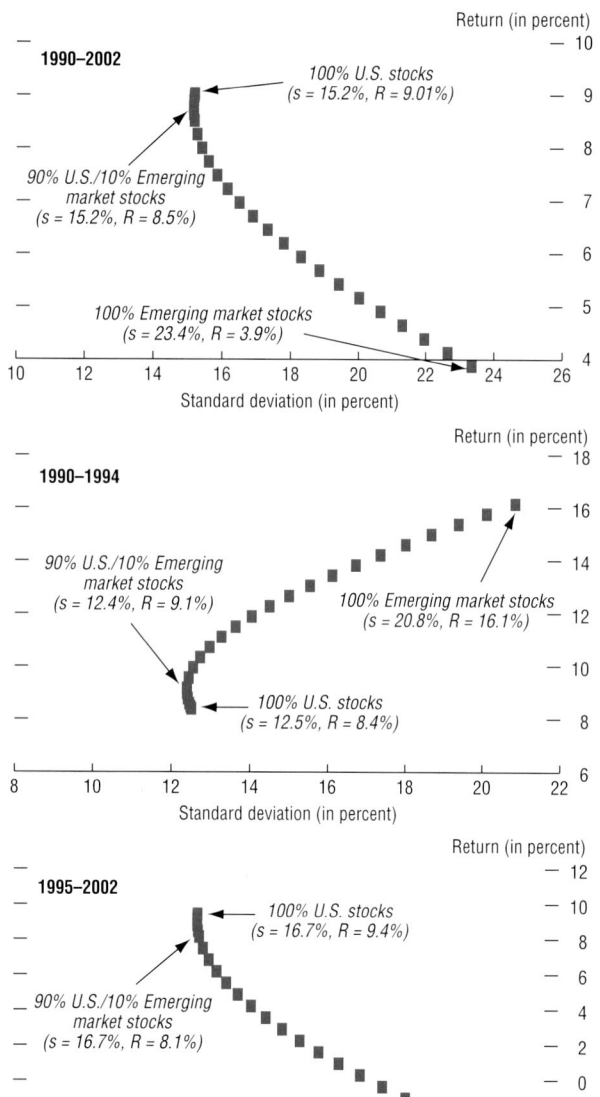

Figure 5. Risk-Return Trade-Off for Combinations of Emerging Market Stocks and U.S. Stocks[1]

Sources: S&P/IFC EMDB; Bloomberg L.P.; and IMF staff calculations.
[1]IFCI Composite total return index is used for emerging market stocks and S&P 500 total return index for U.S. stocks. Risk (in percent) is calculated as the annualized standard deviation of monthly returns and return (in percent) as the annualized geometric average of monthly returns.

have been inefficient—negative 3.7 percent return for the highest portfolio risk (24.7 percent). In contrast, U.S. stocks experienced the highest portfolio return for the lowest risk. Portfolio diversification by inclusion of emerging market stocks offered no benefits to global investors in this period.[56]

Explanatory Factors

What accounts for the underperformance of this asset class from a longer-term perspective? The general inclination when seeking explanations of stock market weakness is to search for indicators of overvaluation. But unlike Japan, where long-term stock market weakness has been tied to the overvaluation associated with the bubble in equity prices in the late 1980s, valuations do not appear to be the key factor for explaining the longer-term performance of emerging equity markets. Figure 6 indicates that while the price/earnings ratio for the IFCI Composite has been high during certain episodes, it has on the whole been significantly lower than that of the S&P 500 for much of 1990–2002. Other valuation indicators such as the price-to-book ratio and dividend yields also do not indicate the picture of a structurally overvalued emerging equity market for the entire period.

Market participants argue that the key factor generating both the poor returns on emerging market equities and the reduced diversification benefits has been the experience with financial crises during the second half of the 1990s. A string of financial crises, starting with Mexico in 1995, Asia in 1997–98, Russia in 1998, Brazil in 1999, and, more recently, in Turkey and Argentina, culminated in prominent currency depreciations and severe contractions in the level of economic

[56]Focusing on individual countries rather than the entire index for diversification purposes would not have helped matters. As noted earlier, dedicated emerging market funds have done no better than the index; there has been a high correlation of returns among emerging stock markets through much of the 1990s.

activity in emerging markets. The downturn in economic activity and currency depreciations that accompanied these crises severely weakened both the income and balance sheet position of local corporates, especially in situations where the corporate sector had large foreign currency exposures. Moreover, the restructuring of corporate balance sheets at times involved lengthy negotiations and legal complications that further affected corporate performance. Such poor corporate performance was readily reflected in sharp declines in equity prices, over and above the decline in the value of many emerging market currencies.[57]

The large depreciations associated with these crises also had a strong impact on the returns earned by foreign investors, especially for many emerging equity market funds that tended not to fully hedge their currency exposures. As a result of this experience, foreign investors, whose holdings account for between ¼ and ½ of the market capitalization of some of the largest emerging equity markets, appear to have become more averse to currency risks.

As noted earlier, the second half of the 1990s witnessed a decline in the diversification benefits associated with holding emerging market equities. In part, this reflected the higher correlations between the equity returns in the various countries affected by the emerging market crises. However, this period also saw a trend increase in the correlation between emerging and mature stock returns (Figure 7). This higher correlation related in part to the global effects of some mature market crises (such as the one associated with the failure of Long-Term Capital Management) and the sectoral investment strategies adopted by many global equity investors in connection with the sharp rise and subsequent decline of equity prices in the

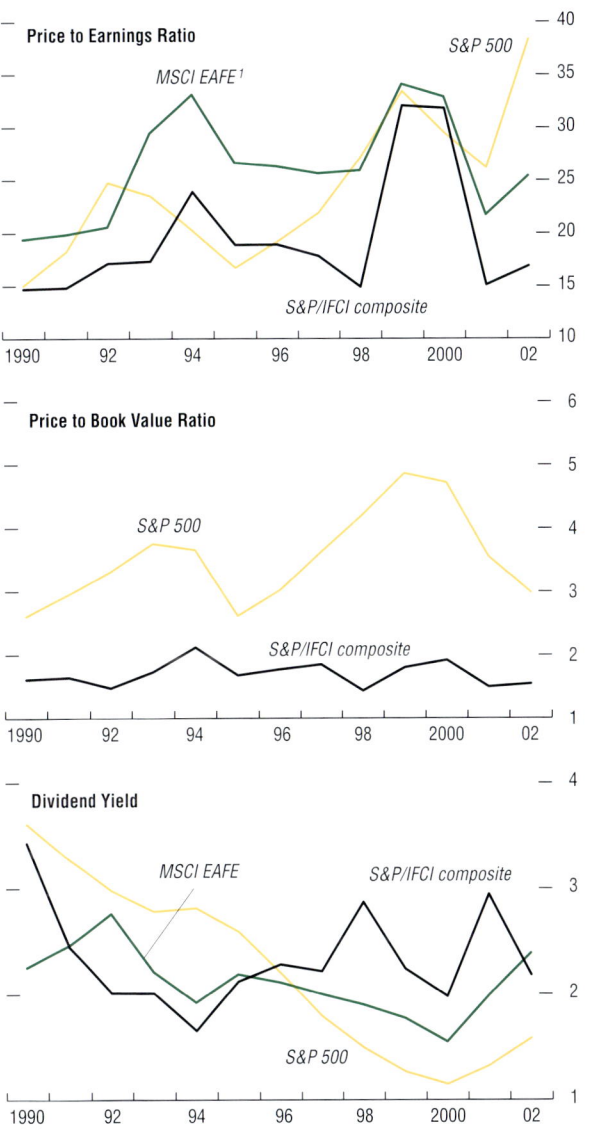

Figure 6. Valuation Indicators in Emerging Equity Markets

Sources: Bloomberg L.P.; and Standard and Poor's.
[1]EAFE stands for Europe, Australia, and Far East.

[57]For instance, while the Thai baht depreciated by 38 percent over the 12 months to May 1998, the stock market declined by 66 percent in U.S. dollar terms; similarly, the Indonesian rupiah depreciated by 78 percent over that same period, while the dollar value of the stock market fell by 88 percent.

CHAPTER III EMERGING EQUITY MARKETS

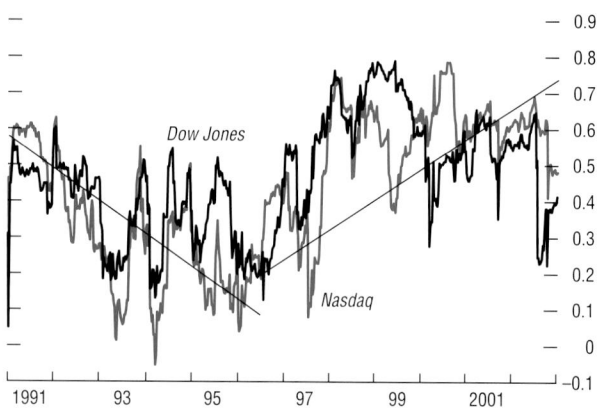

Figure 7. Correlations Between Returns in Emerging and U.S. Equity Markets

Sources: Bloomberg L.P.; and IMF staff calculations.

technology, media, and telecommunications (TMT) sector in the latter part of the 1990s (see Brooks and Catão, 2001).

While crises in emerging and mature markets affected the relative performance of emerging equity markets in the first and second halves of the 1990s, there are certain structural weaknesses that influenced equity market performance throughout the decade, although they became more evident to investors during periods of weak performance. In particular, liquidity, asymmetric information, and corporate governance considerations have had a dampening effect on the performance of emerging market equities. In many emerging markets, a few prominent companies constitute the bulk of the market capitalization of country indexes put out by the IFC and MSCI, and quite often the free float constitutes a small fraction of the companies' market capitalization. Firms included in these indices often tend to be privatized utilities, natural resource and transportation-related companies, or banks, which continue to maintain direct or indirect links to the state and have limited opportunities for future growth. Also, foreign investors worry that adjustments in their holdings of these stocks will lead to large price movements, as the size of the free float is quite small relative to total market capitalization. Generating high returns in emerging equity markets therefore requires going beyond these companies, and picking out-of-index companies with good growth prospects. Market participants argue that many such publicly listed companies do exist, and have attractive valuations, particularly in Asia, where price/earnings ratios on the IFCI index are often much higher than that of the corresponding local index.[58]

---

[58]For instance, the Thai component of the IFCI has a price earnings ratio of 35 currently, while it is about 10 on the local stock market index; in Malaysia, the local stock market price-earnings ratio is 22, while the IFCI component of the country index has a price/earnings ratio of 52.

However, foreign investors do not generally invest in out-of-index stocks either because of liquidity considerations or simply because they are unaware of the potential of these stocks, since international investment banks do not include them in their research coverage.

Issues of transparency and corporate governance have also weighed negatively on emerging market equity performance. In many emerging markets, analysts have concerns about the accuracy and transparency of corporate earnings reports—especially for the case of closely held companies—and asset managers distrust analysts' research. Indeed, in a recent survey (Montagu-Pollock, 2001), a large majority of fund managers (76 percent of the sample) responded that they were not happy with the independence of the research they got from investment banks. Poor corporate governance has been identified as one of the causes of the recent Asian financial crises (see, for instance, Claessens, Djankov, and Lang, 1998), with ownership largely concentrated in the hands of families and the state, in part through the use of pyramid structures, deviations from one-share-one-vote rules, cross holdings, and the appointment of managers and directors who are related to the controlling family. Also, the need to attract strategic investors during the privatization processes of the 1990s in some European and Latin American countries was accompanied by weak minority rights that contributed to abuses from controlling shareholders. Over the past few years, several emerging markets have approved capital market laws that include measures aimed at strengthening minority rights and improving corporate governance and transparency.

The migration of the listings of top-quality emerging market corporates to major mature market financial centers has also taken a toll on the liquidity of emerging equity markets. A common way of raising equity capital in international markets is to issue depository receipts that trade in the United States (American Depository Receipts or ADRs) or in the rest of the world (Global Depository Receipts or GDRs).[59] In general, companies list on a local exchange initially and then offer part of their equity to international investors through depository receipts. During the 1990s emerging market issuers raised on average $7 billion a year through ADRs, but issuance levels in recent years have averaged around $22 billion—though that includes the peak year of 2000. Latin America entities were the most active issuers of ADRs in the early 1990s, but more recently the focus has shifted to Asia. In the early 1990s, about 60 percent of international equity issues took the form of ADRs; this has risen to almost 80 percent in the past three years, with Latin American issues being almost exclusively in the form of depository receipt programs. Market participants argue that for some prominent Latin American stocks, price discovery is done in New York rather than in the local markets.[60]

Along with ADRs, the delisting of stocks from local stock exchanges in emerging markets has also had a negative impact on the asset class. Delisting has been a significant problem in Central Europe, Latin America, and South Africa. In Hungary, for instance, a number of companies have delisted from the local stock exchanges because they have been taken over by multinationals—in 1999, FDI firms accounted for 50 percent of book value added in the nonfinancial business. Similarly, a large number of delistings by foreign companies of their Argentine subsidiaries accounts for a large fraction of the fall in the country's stock exchange market capitalization. In South Africa, some local companies

---

[59]See Box 3.6 in the IMF (2000) for a more extensive discussion of depository receipts programs.
[60]Indeed, the typical risk-return profile of ADRs is not very different from that of locally listed stocks because of arbitrage.

decided to migrate and list abroad to take advantage of the larger investor base and overcome the size limitations of the local market. Delistings have been less of an issue in Asia. A number of prominent companies listed in the local stock exchanges are state-linked, and even in the case of purely private companies, the urge to delist from the local stock exchanges has been precluded by a mixture of nationalism and subtle political pressure.

Implications for Capital Flows

The sustained poor performance of local emerging market equities has sharply altered the global investor base for emerging market equities. For example, dedicated emerging market mutual funds have in some cases witnessed declines in assets under management of one-half. The role of crossover investors, such as pension funds and insurance companies, and tactical investors, such as hedge funds, has increased, and their focus is on opportunistic trading. As noted earlier, the robust performance of emerging equity markets since early 2002 has attracted investor focus on this asset class once again, with a number of global investment banks recommending their clients to go overweight on emerging market equities (see Salomon Smith Barney, 2002; and Goldman Sachs, 2002). As tactical investing in emerging equity markets gains in relative importance, it is likely to accentuate the already volatile net inflows into emerging equity markets. And such a prospective increase in volatility is also likely to have spillover effects into other emerging asset markets, particularly to the currency markets.

Domestic Equity as an Alternative Source of Funding

In response to the emerging market crises of the late 1990s, a number of analysts and policymakers recommended the development of local securities markets as an alternative source of funding for the corporate sector to ameliorate the impact of a banking or external funding crisis. While the emphasis has been largely on the development of local bond markets, the need to reduce the leverage of several large corporates in Asia, combined with the desirability of having more flexible financial structures in volatile environments, has raised the issue of the stock market as a source of finance.

The value of stock market capitalization has been approximately equal, on average, to the value of outstanding bank credit over the last decade in emerging markets (Figure 8). Although this constitutes only a rough approximation of the pattern of corporate finance in emerging markets, it shows the relative importance of equity financing. There are significant differences, however, across time and regions. Bank credit is much larger than equity market capitalization in Asia, while the opposite applies to Latin America and Central Europe. The collapse in equity prices in Asia in 1997 and 1998 accounts for a large share of the fall in market capitalization during these years, and the TMT-led rebound in valuations across the whole spectrum of emerging markets in 1999 explains the reverse phenomenon during that year. Outstanding bank credit grows steadily during the decade in Central Europe and Asia (with the exception of Asia only in 1997), while it flattens out in Latin America after 1994.

In contrast to the similar orders of magnitude in the stocks of debt and equity, bank lending has dominated domestic equity issuance in emerging markets. Between 1990 and 2002, the size of bank flows has been approximately 10 times the size of the equity flows (Figure 9, upper panel). However, volatility has also been substantially greater. This is explained in part by the fact that bank lending is short term and hence needs to be rolled over, while equity is, generally speaking, a permanent source of finance. Nevertheless, the flow data show that, while relatively small in absolute size, equity finance was a relatively resilient source of finance during the Asian crisis. The sharp fall in domestic equity issuance between 2000–02 raises doubts, however, about the long-term prospects of initial public offerings in local markets going forward, an issue that is related to the internationalization of equity markets. As Figure 9 (lower panel) shows, international equity issuance has dominated local equity issuance over 2000–02. Despite that, international equity issuance in emerging markets itself has declined in recent years, with the decline being particularly precipitous in Latin America, related in part to the slowing down of the privatization process (Figures 10 and 11).

While the internationalization of equity markets has helped top-quality emerging market corporates to raise capital at a lower cost, it may thwart efforts to develop local equity markets as an alternative source of finance. The trend toward the internationalization of equity markets is a result of the dramatic reduction in transaction costs associated with improvements in information and computation technologies.[61] The associated reduction in the cost of raising capital in the most advanced exchanges, combined with the integration of capital markets, has made evident the inefficiencies existent in several local emerging equity markets. Several of these markets are reducing listing requirements and other costs associated with initial public offerings, and they are establishing alliances with other exchanges to increase the investor base for local issues (see below for a more detailed discussion). It remains unclear if these local efforts could compensate global trends toward the consolidation of equity market activity in the most efficient financial centers. However, the poor performance of local emerging equity markets during the second half of the 1990s is not necessarily a harbinger of future

[61]The trend toward internationalization of equity markets, which includes delistings, ADR issuance, dual listings and other phenomena, is discussed in IMF (2000); the shift of liquidity toward financial centers and consolidation of exchanges is described in IMF (2001).

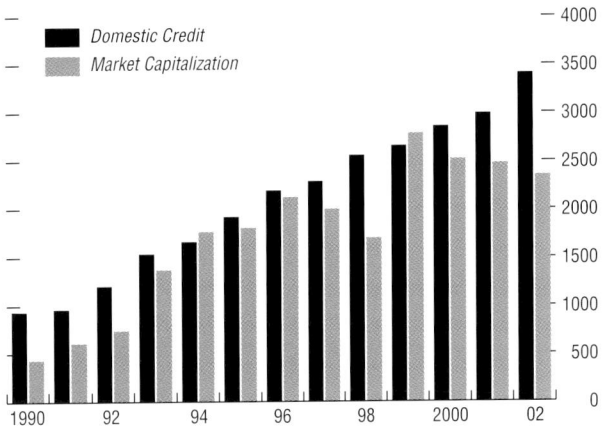

Figure 8. Stock Market Capitalization and Bank Credit
(In billions of U.S. dollars)

Sources: International Monetary Fund, *International Financial Statistics*; and IMF staff estimates.

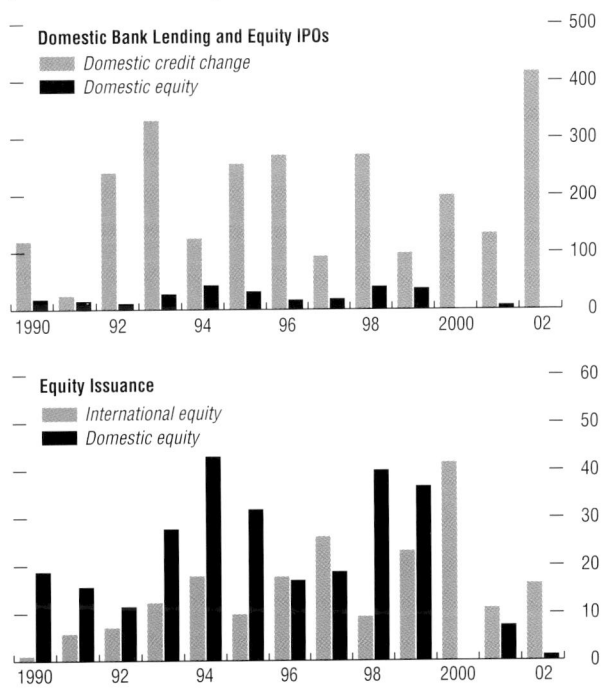

Figure 9. Domestic and International Equity Issuance
(In billions of U.S. dollars)

Sources: International Monetary Fund, *International Financial Statistics*; and IMF staff estimates.

performance. A more stable macroeconomic environment and improved corporate governance and transparency would nonetheless be key elements in furthering the development of these markets. In this regard, the ADRs and GDR programs of emerging market corporates are also likely to play important roles in helping improve corporate transparency and governance.

Stock Exchanges: Developments and Issues in Emerging Markets

Stock exchanges worldwide have been under pressure in recent years. The bear market in equities has shrunk trading volumes literally everywhere and reduced the earnings potential of many exchanges. Moreover, the growth of large automated trading platforms known as electronic communications networks (ECNs) have also put pressure on floor-based trading exchanges. Their capacity to process large quantities of information faster has meant that they have offered less expensive access to buyers and sellers of financial assets than traditional exchanges do. In many industries, pressures of this kind usually lead to a spate of mergers and acquisitions, as firms try to consolidate to compete better in a difficult environment. In stock exchanges, however, mergers and acquisitions have been less prominent, for reasons discussed at greater length below, and the industry has continued to face turmoil.

The pressures faced by stock exchanges in emerging markets (which is the focus of this chapter) have been even more acute in recent years. In addition to the bear market in equities, a drop in IPOs associated with the reduction in privatization and a spate of delistings have called into question the viability of many stock exchanges in emerging markets. Moreover, the drying up of liquidity associated with these developments has meant that the role of the stock market in intermediating finances for economic development has been dented to some extent, which has the poten-

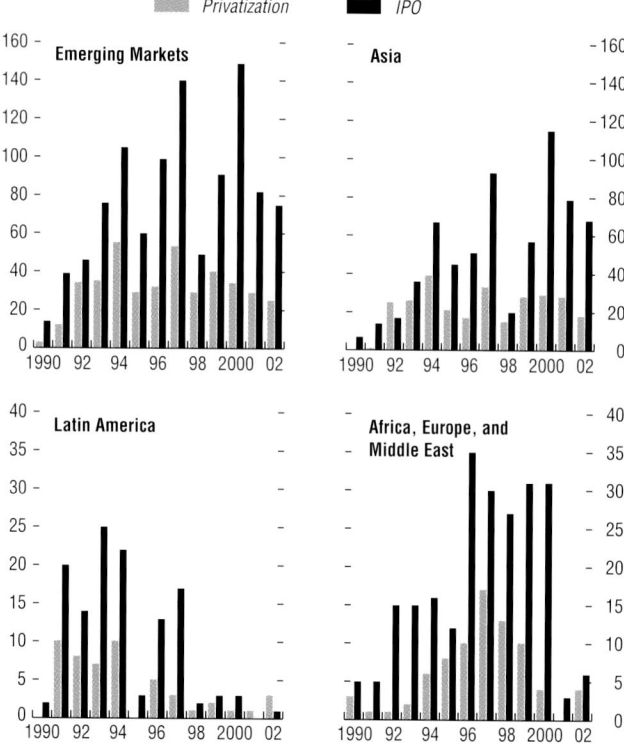

Figure 10. International Equity Issuance by IPO and Privatization
(In numbers)

Sources: Dealogic; and IMF staff estimates.

tial to create difficulties of a systemic nature in many emerging market economies. This is particularly important, given the findings of recent research that the combined financial intermediation effects of stock markets and banks have a statistically and economically large positive impact on economic growth—with the extent of the development of stock markets having a positive effect on economic growth that is independent of the impact due to banks.[62]

In view of the favorable impact that deep and liquid stock markets can have on economic growth, it becomes particularly important to have a proper understanding of the forces that have put pressures on stock exchanges in emerging markets. This section carries out such an analysis, and also discusses the response of the various stock exchanges to the difficulties that they face.

Stock Exchanges Under Pressure

As discussed in the previous sections, emerging market equities have not only underperformed mature market equities in recent years, but also posted negative returns. Moreover, global equity portfolios that include emerging market equities have offered little in the way of diversification benefits over the past five years. Given this difficult environment, it is not surprising to find that stock exchanges in emerging markets have faced acute pressures on profit margins.

The underperformance of the equity market by itself need not necessarily have to compress profit margins of stock exchanges, however. If trading volumes are sufficiently high, because investors resort to reshuffling their portfolios frequently to deal with an environment of low or negative returns, then the stock exchange as an entity should be less

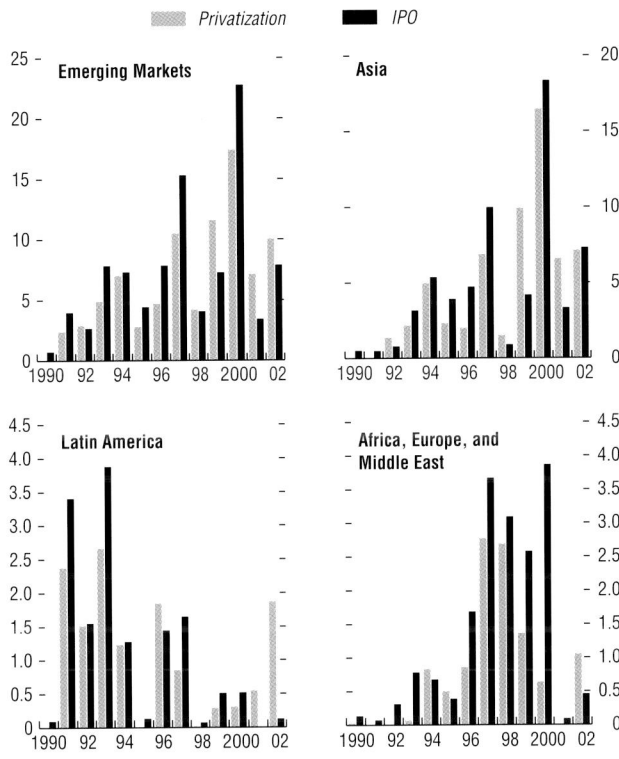

Figure 11. International Equity Issuance by IPO and Privatization
(In billions of U.S. dollars)

Sources: Dealogic; and IMF staff estimates.

---

[62]See, for instance, Beck and Levine (2001). They argue that stock markets act as an offset to the monopoly power exercised by banks, and the competitive nature of the stock markets encourages innovative growth-enhancing activities as opposed to the more conservative intermediation approach of banks.

Figure 12. Monthly Dollar Trading Volume for Selected Asian Countries
(In billions of U.S. dollars)

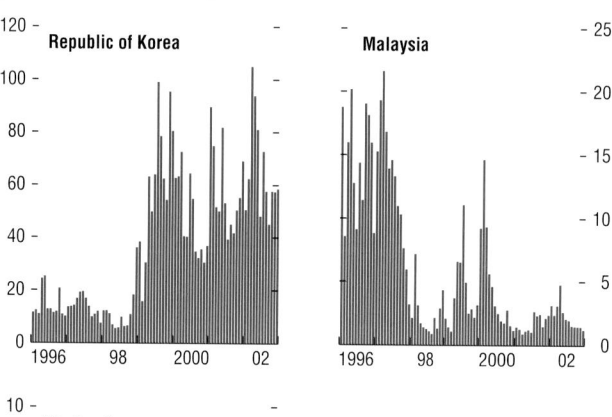

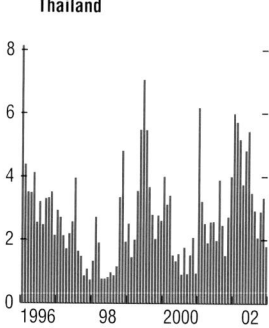

Source: Standard and Poor's.

adversely affected than holders of equities. But as can be seen from Figures 12–14, trading volumes in many prominent emerging markets have declined sharply in recent years, with the decline being particularly precipitous in countries such as Malaysia, Argentina, Brazil, Hungary, and Poland.

While the decline in trading volumes has provided the essential backdrop for the pressures faced by the stock exchanges in emerging markets, other factors have accentuated these pressures. The deregulation of brokerage commissions has increased the competitive pressures on the exchanges, particularly where profit margins were maintained through a mixture of barriers to entry and antiquated trading and governance structures. The fact that many of the exchanges in emerging markets tend to be member owned has been a factor that has obstructed the technological evolution of electronic trading. Many of the members of these exchanges came from small brokerages and could not afford the fixed costs involved in instituting ECNs, but resisted takeovers by bigger players who had the capacity to restructure. Notable exceptions to this pattern have been the stock and derivatives exchanges of Hong Kong SAR, which merged and demutualized, and the stock exchange of Singapore, where shares were offered not only to the existing members of the exchanges but also to banks and other institutional investors. These developments allowed a radical restructuring of these exchanges and made possible a more flexible and efficient organizational structure for trading. As a result, these exchanges are now playing the role of regional hubs with many prominent companies in Asian countries preferring to list in the exchanges of Hong Kong SAR and Singapore. While there has been consolidation of the stock exchanges in many emerging markets (through, for instance, the merging regional exchanges within a country, as in Brazil), the process of demutualization and instituting ECNs has been somewhat patchy when compared with the changes that have taken place in Hong Kong SAR and Singapore.

As noted briefly in the earlier sections, stock exchanges in emerging markets have also been buffeted by declines in the number of IPOs, the increasing tendency of some prominent companies to take the ADR/GDR route, and the delisting of companies altogether from local markets as they get acquired by multinationals. These developments, which have been largely confined to Latin America and Central Europe, but which have also cropped up in Asia more recently, are discussed immediately below. The steps taken by the various stock exchanges to respond to these pressures is explored later in this chapter.

The stock market and the exchanges in Central Europe were kept buoyant by a wave of privatizations during 1995–97 (see Box 5 for the Russian experience). Once the initial privatizations were completed, a number of smaller companies came on stream and issued IPOs, particularly during 1999–2000. The IPO market has dried up, however, particularly in Hungary and Poland during the last two years—for instance, there were no IPOs issued in Hungary in 2001. A number of companies have preferred to take on a strategic investor rather than go through the IPO route. In addition to the paucity of IPOs, liquidity in the exchanges of Central Europe has been reduced by delistings than by local firms taking the ADR/GDR route. In Hungary, in particular, multinational participation in the economy is substantial, and a number of local firms have delisted from the local exchanges as they have been taken over by multinationals. All of this has raised the issue of the viability of the stock exchanges in Central Europe.

In Latin America, the string of financial crises since the mid-1990s has constituted the essential backdrop under which the stock exchanges have found themselves under pressure. As in Central Europe, the local equity market has not served as an important source of funding for corporates in Latin America

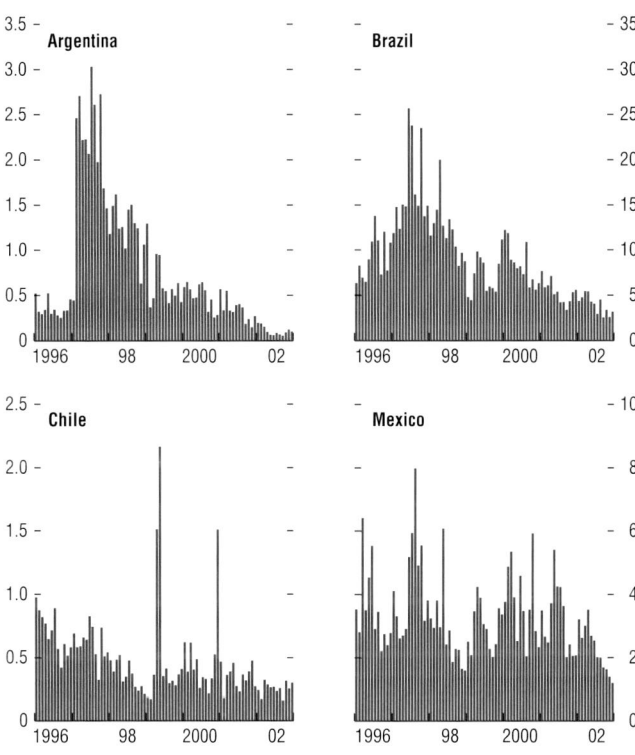

Figure 13. Monthly Dollar Trading Volume for Selected Latin American Countries
(In billions of U.S. dollars)

Source: Standard and Poor's.

CHAPTER III EMERGING EQUITY MARKETS

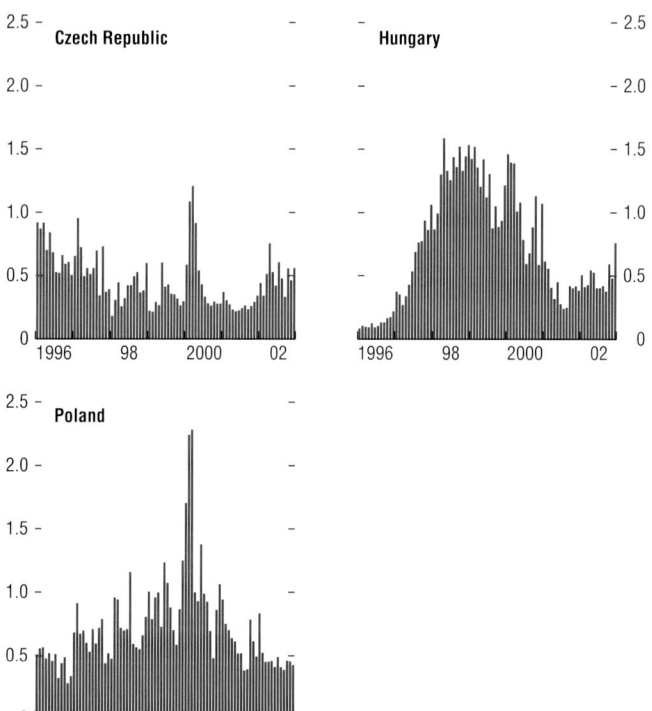

Figure 14. Monthly Dollar Trading Volume for Selected European Countries
(In billions of U.S. dollars)

Source: Standard and Poor's.

during the past few years. For instance, there have been only 10 primary equity issues in Brazil between May 2000 and May 2002, fewer than the number of delistings during this period. However, the pressures on the stock exchanges in Latin America have owed more (in the relative sense) to firms taking the ADR/GDR route than due to delistings. A number of securities taxes in Brazil and capital controls in Chile, for instance, have made listing and trading ADRs in New York more attractive for many firms than listing and trading in the local exchanges.

Stock exchanges in Asia have been under much less pressure than those in Central Europe and Latin America. While the IPO process has slowed in Asia in 2000–02, it has not been battered in the way that it has been in the other emerging market regions. Delisting of companies from the local market and the issue of ADRs/GDRs have also been a less prominent feature of the Asian equity landscape. In Malaysia and Singapore, for instance, many of the listed companies are state linked and are unlikely to be taken over by multinationals and delist from the local market. But even in the case of purely private companies, the urge to delist from the local exchanges is and will be precluded by a mixture of nationalism and subtle political pressure; stock exchanges in Asia are perceived as national symbols, much in the way that national airlines are, and are likely to be bolstered by the state as they face pressures. While private companies in these countries can take the ADR route, they are in general too small for this to be a systematically profitable option.

Factors Driving Companies to take the ADR/GDR Route

Delisting and taking the ADR/GDR route are phenomena that are not just confined to emerging market stock exchanges, but are also pervasive in the case of mature market stock exchanges. While one may expect that as capital market integration proceeds, geography

Box 5. The Equity Market in Russia

The Russian equity market has been one of the best performing stock markets in recent years. Over the last two years the RTSI dollar index has returned about 50 percent annually. Its five-year performance has been even more impressive—returning about 58 percent annually. This rapid growth in stock prices has raised the issue of whether there has been an "irrational exuberance" for Russian stocks. This box offers a brief overview of the institutional framework of the Russian stock market, and provides an analysis of whether the run-up in Russian stock prices is sustainable in terms of fundamentals.

The Structure of the Russian Stock Market

There are two main organized exchanges for trading equities in Russia—the Russian Trading System (RTS) and the Moscow Interbank Currency Exchange (MICEX). The RTS currently includes 386 stocks representing 244 listed companies. The RTS dollar-denominated index, consisting of 59 stocks, is viewed as the benchmark Russian equity index, both locally and internationally. The MICEX, which originally specialized in currency and debt trading, began trading equities in 1997. There are about 200 stocks listed on MICEX, and it is the favorite trading platform of local investors. There is reportedly a high level of leverage used in trading stocks listed on MICEX and pervasive day trading. However, since the price discovery process for stocks takes place in the better managed RTS (with MICEX market makers often using RTS prices as indicative quotes), the high leverage used by MICEX brokers, by itself, has not impinged on valuations in those stocks that are traded in both exchanges.

There are very few restrictions on foreign ownership of Russian equities, and there is no general regulation that limits foreign investor participation in the local equity market. However, there are several special cases. The most prominent example is Gazprom, where nonresidential holdings of the company's share cannot exceed 20 percent of its charter capital. However, the effective ceiling is even lower, as foreign investors can only buy Gazprom ADRs and not the local shares (the total value of ADRs is less than 4 percent of the company's market capitalization). The presence of such restrictions largely explains the sizable ADR premium for Gazprom shares, which does not exist for other Russian stocks. In addition, Gazprom shares can be traded on four exchanges only—the Moscow Stock Exchange, St. Petersburg Stock Exchange, and two other small regional exchanges. Other special cases include shares of UES and Sberbank. The limit on foreign ownership of UES shares is 25 percent, while for Sberbank it is 12 percent.

Valuations

The run-up in Russian stock prices, by itself, does not indicate whether there is a bubble or not. Conceptually, this can be viewed as the obverse of the situation in Japan, or for that matter in the NASDAQ—where stock prices have fallen by about 75 percent from peak levels, but they are still considered by a number of market participants to be overvalued. A straightforward way of looking at the issue of whether the run-up in equity prices in Russia is a source of concern is simply to look at valuations. The price-earnings ratio for the RTSI is currently only about 8–9. The price-earnings ratio for the IFCI (Russia) and MSCI (Russia), indexes that represent investibility for foreign investors is even less—in the range of 6–7. In contrast, the price-earnings ratio for the IFCI Composite, the benchmark dollar based index for emerging market equities is about 15; for the S&P 500 it is about 28. That is, in terms of the price-earnings ratio of the broad stock indexes, the Russian equity market does not look overvalued despite the dramatic run-up in equity prices.

Given that almost 70 percent of the market capitalization of the RTSI is oil related, it is necessary to go beyond macro-valuation measures, such as the price-earnings ratio, and

Box 5 *(concluded)*

look more closely at sectoral valuation measures. In particular, it is necessary to evaluate if Russian oil companies are fairly valued or not. The price-earnings ratio has certain limitations as a valuation measure—it does not take the financing structure of companies into account, and also fails to take account of accounting idiosyncrasies, making relative value comparisons difficult. An alternative valuation measure preferred by many analysts for making relative value comparisons is the ratio of the enterprise value to earnings before interest, taxes, dividends, and amortization (EV/EBITDA); enterprise value is defined as the sum of a company's market capitalization and debt.

On an EV/EBITDA measure, Russian oil companies appear cheap on both absolute and relative grounds. Russian oil companies, on average, have an EV/EBITDA of about 2.5, compared to about 4 for some of the prominent oil companies in emerging markets and about 6 for the major oil companies in mature markets. Market participants argue that doing relative value analysis for oil companies is a lot easier than is the case with some other industries—the oil industry produces basically a homogenous commodity with a well-defined production process, and fuzzy concepts such as goodwill do not enter into the valuation process. Market participants also offer other anecdotal evidence to indicate that Russian oil companies, and by implication the stock market as a whole, is still cheap despite the run-up in equity prices; for instance, it has been estimated that Yukos, one of Russia's largest oil companies, has a market capitalization that is about one-third of ChevronTexaco despite producing half its output, having oil reserves that are larger and production costs that are significantly lower. Moreover, market participants note that Russian oil companies are in the process of entering into strategic agreements with foreign oil companies—the recent strategic alliance between BP and TNK, which is expected to ratchet up significantly the inflow of foreign direct investment into Russia, is the most prominent example. Russia is also planning to enhance the pipeline structure with collaboration agreements with both China and Japan, and these developments are expected to add significantly to export capacity of the oil industry and the earnings potential of the Russian oil companies.

Russian metals and telecoms are also evaluated to be cheap when looked at in relation to EV/EBITDA measures for comparable sectors in other emerging markets. Wimm-Bill-Dann's (the food company) successful IPO last year sparked a tremendous interest in Russian consumer good stocks. But market participants note that Wimm-Bill-Dann as well as the other prominent Russian consumer goods companies are not cheap on a relative value basis. Thus, the attractiveness of the Russian equity market essentially appears to be an oil and metals story.

Investor Base

The investor base for Russian equities appears to have evolved and stabilized in a form that is likely to offer support to the stock market. A combination of local investors and foreign dedicated emerging market funds slowly began to increase their exposure to Russian stocks in the first half of 2000, stabilizing a market that had been badly affected by the events of August 1998. In the second half of 2001, a new type of investor—global equity funds with sectoral allocations—started buying up several Russian stocks as part of a relative value play on the global oil and gas sectors—for instance going short on Shell and BP and going long on Yukos and Sibneft. Traditional global equity funds with country allocations have also started to evince an interest in the Russian market. These are typically conservative equity funds—their mandates warrant a time-consuming approval process before they can enter a new market—but once they enter the market it tends to be a relatively longer-term commitment. While hedge fund activity in Russian equities picked up last year, they have been late comers into the stock market, unlike in the case of eurobonds where they got in early and made considerable gains.

The entry of the global equity funds, along with MSCI's decision to increase Russia's weighting in its Emerging Market Free index, has been another factor supportive of the Russian equity market. As a result of the MSCI index rebalancing, the weight of Russia in the EMF index has risen to about 4 percent, roughly the same weight as India. Market participants expect MSCI to broaden the set of companies that it includes in its Russia index (primarily with additions from the telecoms sector), and this is expected to draw in more foreign investors into the Russian equity market. Investor interest is also likely to be perked up by a number of IPOs coming on stream in the years ahead.

Divestment of state shares in Russia is not expected to weigh down on the stock market in the way that it has in China, for instance. Unlike in China, where the state owns about two-thirds of the market capitalization in the equity market, the ownership structure of the Russian equity market is more diverse. Except in the case of notable exceptions such as Gazprom, UES, and Sberbank, radical privatization was essentially completed by 1996 in Russia. Ownership in many of the important companies are distributed among management, employees, strategic owners, and foreigners. Moreover, Russia does not have to privatize for fiscal reasons, and divestment in companies where the state has significant ownership can be done in a more controlled way by taking into account market timing. Nevertheless, despite the favorable fundamentals for Russian equities, concerns about corporate governance issues are likely to cap the upside potential for the stock market.

could become increasingly irrelevant to the process of raising finance, that does not seem to have happened in practice. The number of companies seeking a foreign listing has increased throughout the 1990s both in emerging markets and the mature markets of Europe. Exchanges in the United States have been the main beneficiaries of this trend. Companies tend to cross list in the more liquid and larger markets, and in markets where companies from their industry are already cross listed, and this makes the exchanges of the United States a natural destination for many firms. In response to this business opportunity, U.S. exchanges and regulators have made a concerted effort to reduce regulatory costs and facilitate foreign listings. For instance, in the early 1990s the Securities and Exchange Commission in the United States became significantly more cooperative toward non-U.S. companies trying to register in the United States; this change in attitude was apparently prompted by stock exchange officials who regarded the listings of foreign companies as an attractive business opportunity for themselves.

A number of recent academic studies have used panel data for identifying the driving forces of cross listing, and their conclusions throw important light on why many firms in emerging markets choose to take the ADR/GDR route (see, in this context, Pagano and others, 2001). The need for greater liquidity appears to be one of the most important factors in the decision to cross list, and explains why the exchanges of the United States have become the popular destinations for firms in emerging markets to list in. The larger size of the stock market not only provides access to a larger pool of potential investors, but being listed on a large stock market can confer greater visibility and reputation for a company.

Cross-listing decisions also appear to be influenced by informational cascades—i.e., by wanting to be where the peers are. If a company's managers observe many competitors listing on a particular stock exchange, they are likely to infer that there might be advantages from imitating them, and are likely to cross list in a bigger and more liquid stock exchange, even when there may be no pressing economic requirement to do so. This competitive pressure to issue ADRs/GDRs may in part explain the extent of the pressures that stock exchanges in emerging markets have been confronted with in recent years. The discrepancy in accounting standards between the home country and the host country also appears to play a role in the decision to cross list. Listing in a country with better accounting standards allows the company to precommit to greater transparency and reduces the monitoring costs of its shareholders and their required rate of return. However, if the discrepancy in accounting standards between the home and the host country is too large, then the discrepancy may actually negatively affect the decisions of some firms to cross list. Another possible benefit of cross listing is to expose the company to the attention of additional financial analysts, and thereby to a wider investor base. However, in practice, academic studies do not find analyst coverage to be a significant explanatory factor of the decision to cross list.

The Response of the Stock Exchanges

Stock exchanges (both in emerging and mature markets) have responded in a variety of ways to deal with the pressures that they have been subjected to in recent years. For instance, some stock exchanges have decided to go public. Prominent examples are the London Stock Exchange and the Deutsche Borse. Going public has allowed these exchanges to mobilize funds for upgrading their ECNs and acquiring the capacity to compete better with rival exchanges. In other cases stock exchanges have sought alliances with each other to enhance liquidity. Prominent examples of this are Euronext—which is an alliance of the Paris, Amsterdam, and Brussels exchanges; Newex—which is an alliance of the Deutsche and Vienna Borses; and Norex—which is an alliance of the exchanges in Copenhagen, Stockholm, Oslo, and Iceland. The process of forming alliances to survive appears to be still in its infancy among emerging stock exchanges. Particularly in the case of the Asian exchanges, where stock exchanges tend to be local monopolies, the pressure to consolidate in response to technological innovation has been much less than for exchanges in the United States; it has been estimated, for instance, that the number of stock exchanges in the United States came down from over a 100 in the nineteenth century to about five major stock exchanges currently in response to the competitive pressures exerted by tehnological innovation (see Shy and Tarkka, 2001).

In Central Europe, the Warsaw stock exchange has taken strides to restructure. The Warsaw stock exchange, which is the biggest in the region, is now a fully electronic order driven market and has instituted a number of new rules to make trading transparent. The exchange has been in talks with Euronext to form a loose alliance and has aspirations to become a regional hub in Central Europe for trading equities. The Budapest stock exchange has put in place plans to demutualize and list as a public company. To make mergers and acquisitions possible, the Hungarian administration has abolished the rule that limits individual ownership to no more than 10 percent of the exchange. The Budapest stock exchange has also recently instituted talks with both Euronext and the London Stock Exchange for forming a loose partnership; it intends, however, to maintain its independence. The Czech stock exchange has also come up with plans to demutualize.

Local stock exchanges in Latin America have also taken a number of steps to revive activity and make themselves viable entities. In Brazil, the São Paulo Stock Exchange (BOVESPA) has introduced a new market— O Novo Mercado—available only to companies meeting stricter rules on corporate governance. The Novo Mercado is a listing segment designed for trading shares issued by companies that voluntarily undertake to abide by good practices of corporate governance and disclosure requirements that go beyond those already requested by Brazilian legislation. It is hoped that this would reduce the pressure for companies wanting to delist for "reputational" reasons. In Chile, the Stock Exchange of Santiago has recently launched the Mercado Emergente, a new segment for "emerging enterprises." Recently established firms with innovative business plans and a potential for strong growth can receive financial assistance for the registration of costs and list in the local stock exchange. Despite the measures taken by the stock exchanges in Latin America, many analysts consider the liquidity problem to be serious, particularly in Chile, where the reforms are viewed as having come too late to bring liquidity back into the stock markets.

As already noted, the stock exchanges in Asia have been under relatively less pressure than those in other emerging markets. In particular, the exchanges of Hong Kong SAR and Singapore have already completed the process of demutualizing and going public and are in relatively good shape to face the challenges ahead. The stock exchanges in Singapore and Australia have recently formed an alliance that allows them to trade in each other's exchanges. A full-fledged merger of these two exchanges is seen as being unlikely for nationalistic reasons; moreover, a merger is not seen as necessary for developing the equity asset class in these two countries. The Thai stock exchange perceives cross-border trading of stocks between it and the other regional exchanges, rather than cross-border listing, as a preferred option. This is also true of the Malaysian stock exchange. Here, there is an essential asymmetry between Singapore and the other countries in the region—whereas Singapore would like to function as the regional hub, its neighboring stock exchanges are less interested in losing their distinctive identities. The stock exchanges in China are relatively new, and despite the fact that a number of Chinese companies have been listing in Hong Kong SAR and Singapore, they have not been subject to the same kind of pressures seen in other emerging markets (see Box 6). In fact, with firms queuing up to list in the Shanghai exchange, the exchange can afford to be sanguine about Chinese firms listing abroad; the Shanghai stock exchange foresees a situation in which dual listing becomes the norm for many Chinese firms. The Korean stock exchange, which is currently run as a self-regulating nonprofit organization that provides a trading platform for stocks, bond index futures, and options, also appears to have no immediate plans to demutualize.

Conclusions

Emerging market equities can provide global investors with attractive absolute returns as well as an avenue for diversifying their portfolios. The evidence indicates that investors reaped such benefits in the first half of the 1990s, but that the gains disappeared between 1995 and 2001. This deterioration in the performance of emerging market equities gave rise to tactical investors, whose opportunistic behavior is likely to increase the volatility of capital inflows into emerging markets. The underperformance of emerging market equities from a longer-term perspective does not appear to be primarily due to overvaluation, though price/earnings ratios in emerging market equities have been high in some years. Some of the main factors in this underperformance are (1) a string of financial crises, starting with Mexico in 1994, that has drastically pruned the U.S. dollar returns on emerging market equities; (2) concerns about corporate transparency and governance; and (3) the growing importance of American Depository Receipts (ADRs) and delistings, which has also reduced the universe of liquid stocks in emerging markets and has thinned both the domestic and global investor base. While the stocks of debt and equity are of similar sizes, bank lending has dominated domestic equity issuance in emerg-

Box 6. The Equity Market in China

The stock market in China has grown rapidly since the mid-1990s, with market capitalization rising dramatically from less than 10 percent of GDP in 1995 to about 40 percent currently (see Figure). This rapid growth reflects the greater role in China's reform process given to capital markets by the Chinese authorities since the 15th Party Congress in September 1997. Beginning at that time, the authorities decided to increase listings on both the domestic and international stock markets to help finance the cost of enterprise restructuring, impose greater market discipline on state-owned enterprises, and develop a market for allocating savings to the most productive uses. Domestic investors with ample savings and relatively few investment opportunities responded enthusiastically to official efforts to encourage stock ownership, and currently a sizable segment of households in China have some stake in the stock market. The institutional structure of the Chinese stock market is complex, given the multifaceted objectives involved in developing it, and a brief description of this structure is provided below.

The Structure of the Equity Market

The stock market in China is highly segmented. The A share market was initially open to Chinese residents only. In 2002 it was also open to qualified investors abroad. It consists of about 1,200 listed companies currently, and is investible in local currency only. The B share market began in 1992 to allow foreigners to participate in the Chinese equity market by investing in foreign currency only. There are currently about 111 companies listed on the B share market. In practice, the B share market has been dominated by Chinese nationals, who have in the past used regulatory loopholes to invest part of their considerable holdings of foreign currency in this market. Chinese nationals have officially been allowed to invest in the B share market since February 2001 and they account for almost 95 percent of share holdings in this market currently. There is also the H share market, which trades shares of Chinese companies listed in Hong Kong SAR and other stock exchanges outside of China. Almost 80 percent of the IPOs in Hong Kong SAR in 2001 came from China. The links between the Chinese and Hong Kong SAR equity markets are, in fact, much deeper than indicated by the importance of H shares. "Red Chips" are companies incorporated in Hong Kong SAR, but whose substantial shareholders and production bases are in China—the combination of H shares and "Red Chips" now constitutes about 30 percent of the Hong Kong SAR stock market.

Performance of the Stock Market

After experiencing rapid growth in the latter half of the 1990s, equity prices witnessed a sustained decline, starting in mid-2001 (see the Figure). Despite the pickup in recent months, the A share market is down by about 20 percent and the B share market by about 40 percent from the highs of mid-2001. What are the factors weighing on the Chinese stock market currently? Is the decline a rational response to unsustainable valuations, or are we witnessing a bout of irrational panic?

Valuations in the A share market currently reflect price-earnings ratio of 30 to 40; this is almost twice the price-earnings ratio in the B share market. The substantial divergence in valuations between the A and the B share markets is due to segmentation—the driving forces of equity prices in the two markets are different and arbitrage between the two is highly imperfect. Many market participants argue that even these high valuations do not fully capture the extent to which the market is overvalued. For example, many of the companies initially listed in the A share market were state-linked enterprises, a number of them in "sunset sectors," with limited prospects for a significant improvement in earnings potential. Moreover, a part of the earnings of some companies listed in the A share market comes from profits obtained from stock market spec-

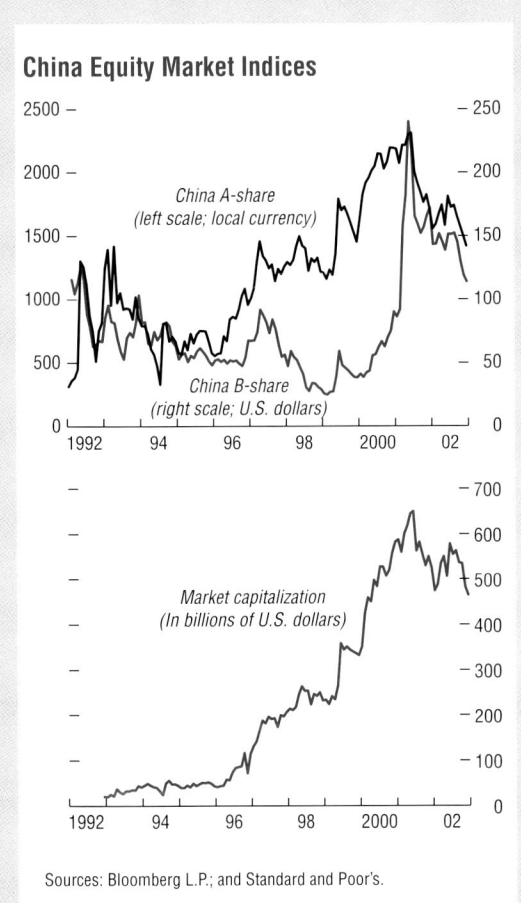

China Equity Market Indices

Sources: Bloomberg L.P.; and Standard and Poor's.

ulation. And this type of profit will disappear as the market subsides.

Investor Base

Almost 90 percent of the investor base for equities in China is retail. Households in China have been confronted with limited opportunities available for investment, other than to hold deposits in banks. Consequently, a sizable part of household savings was placed in the stock market, and these investments have been a key factor driving stock prices. The unease over high valuations among retail investors appears to have been mitigated partly by the fact that many companies are state-linked, generating plausible expectations of a bail-out in the strategically important companies. The institutional investor base has developed only recently, largely as a consequence of official action to promote it. Mutual funds in China are not strictly equity-based or bond-based, but instead invest in a mixture of equities and fixed-income products. In contrast to the retail segment of the market, institutional investors have been more wary of current valuations and are at present largely in bonds or cash. Foreign investors wanting an exposure to the Chinese equity market have traded primarily H shares rather than B shares, because of the more stringent transparency requirements in the former market. Foreign investors appear to be even more concerned than local investors about both the high valuations in the Chinese equity market and the prospects of an increase in the supply of shares (the concerns about the supply-side effects appear to have been mitigated somewhat after the announcement in June 2002 that the divestment process is likely to slow—see below for details), and this in turn has depressed the equity market in Hong Kong SAR.

The Primary Market—the Initial Public Offering (IPO) Process

Market analysts argue that the IPO process in China was initially focused on generating revenues through privatization for the state. More recently, a number of what market participants regard as more viable companies have been brought to the market. Nevertheless, the idea of an IPO as a fund-raising process for the state rather than as a resource allocation mechanism continues to find resonance in China. After a decline of about 30 percent in the value of IPOs in 2001, about 55 billion yuan of IPOs came on stream in 2002—a slight increase over 2001. In contrast to early IPOs, which were mainly in the manufacturing sector, the next batch of IPOs are likely to also involve banks and insurance companies, which need to be strengthened ahead of the competitive challenges linked to WTO accession.

Box 6 *(concluded)*

An IPO in China can be a complex and lengthy process. Companies intending to issue IPOs should in the first instance have been in existence for at least three years and should have generated profits in the three years prior to listing. They have to accept guidance from local investment banks on the modalities of functioning as publicly listed, and the entire process from the intention to list publicly to the beginning of secondary trading can take up to a year to complete. Moreover, until the restrictions were removed recently, there was a quota system for IPOs, with each province being offered a choice of four to five companies to list on an initial public offer waiting list. This policy was cancelled recently. A number of companies have chosen to take the quicker route of listing in Hong Kong SAR and Singapore.

Some technical requirements of the IPO process in China have resulted in the building up of speculative pressures in the equity market. When companies list in the local stock market, a "rule-of-thumb" is applied to cap the price of the stock to generate a historical price earnings ratio of about 20 to 25. Given that the average price earnings ratio in the A share market is about 40, those with access to the IPOs can generate substantial profits when secondary trading in the newly listed shares begins. To minimize abuse of the system, the IPO allocations are made according to a formula, whereby the allocation is a function of the holding period—that is, those willing to hold on to the IPOs for longer periods get more stock allocated.

Regulatory Initiatives

The authorities have taken a number of steps recently to strengthen the functioning of the stock markets in China. The China Securities Regulatory Commission has embarked on a broad initiative to improve transparency by cracking down on fraud and market manipulation, issued tighter rules to delist loss-making enterprises, and imposed more stringent disclosure and accounting requirements on listed companies. They have also required listed companies to have at least one-third of their boards composed of independent directors by 2003.

The biggest challenge for the authorities, however, is to find a way of divesting state shares—both for revenue generating and corporate governance reasons—without disrupting the market. Given that two-thirds of the listed shares in China are currently owned by the state and not traded actively on the secondary market, the expectation of an increase in the supply of shares when restricted shares are freed up is one of the main factors that have roiled markets over the past year. Creating a tracker fund as in Hong Kong SAR to sell state shares is less of a viable option in China, given the magnitude of the delisting needed. The authorities have, however, been cognizant of the delicate supply-demand balance in the stock market, and announced in June 2002 that the plans to divest state shares would be put off for the near future. Instead, the plan is to transfer part of the state's equity holdings to strategic investors through agreement transfers.

ing markets. Between 1990 and 2001, the size of bank lending has been approximately 10 times the size of domestic equity issuance, but the volatility of bank lending has also been substantially greater. Moreover, while relatively small in absolute size, equity finance was a relatively resilient source of finance during the Asian crisis. The sharp fall in domestic equity issuance in 2000 and 2001 raises doubts, however, about the long-term prospects of initial public offerings in local markets as an alternative financing mechanism going forward, an issue that is largely related to the increasing internationalization of equity markets.

CHAPTER IV

THE ROLE OF FINANCIAL DERIVATIVES IN EMERGING MARKETS

Anna Ilyina

Financial derivatives are commonly used for managing various financial risk exposures, including price, foreign exchange, interest rate, and credit risks. By allowing investors to unbundle and transfer these risks, derivatives contribute to a more efficient allocation of capital, facilitate cross-border capital flows, and create more opportunities for portfolio diversification. Thus, financial derivatives are essential for the development of efficient capital markets. However, just like any other complex financial instrument, derivatives may and, in fact, have at times been used by market players to take on excessive risk, avoid prudential safeguards, and manipulate accounting rules. For example, in the absence of adequate internal risk control and prudential supervision, derivative instruments may allow a company to take on excessive leverage by shifting certain exposures off balance sheets. Although the problem of misuse of derivatives is perceived to be more acute in emerging market countries where prudential regulation, credit information infrastructure, and risk management practices are not fully developed, it is certainly not limited to these countries. In a world of constantly evolving financial instruments, the design of prudential regulations that create incentives for market participants to use derivatives appropriately remains one of the biggest challenges for regulators in both mature and emerging markets.

This chapter provides an overview of local derivatives markets in emerging economies and focuses on two issues: how the use of derivatives facilitated capital flows to emerging economies and what was the role of derivatives in past emerging market crises.

Overview of Derivatives Markets in Emerging Economies

Despite rapid growth over the past several years, emerging market derivatives account for only 1 percent of the total outstanding notionals in global derivatives markets. Local derivatives markets in emerging economies differ greatly in their sizes, both in absolute terms and relative to cash markets. Compared with mature markets, the ratio of outstanding notional value of derivatives to market capitalization of the underlying asset markets is fairly small in most emerging economies (see Table 9). The most common problems that constrain the development of local derivatives markets are (1) relatively underdeveloped markets for underlying instruments; (2) weak/inadequate legal and market infrastructure, and (3) restrictions on the use of derivatives by local and foreign entities.

Currency Derivatives

Most of the currency derivatives trading around the world takes place in the over-the-counter (OTC) markets, with foreign exchange swaps accounting for more than two-thirds of the turnover. The turnover in global currency markets followed a declining trend from 1998 and up until early 2001 due to the introduction of the euro, expansion of E-broking, and banking sector consolidation. By contrast, during the same period, the turnover in the emerging foreign exchange spot and derivatives markets increased, with the share of emerging market currencies (including the Hong Kong SAR and Singapore dollars) in the global foreign exchange spot market turnover rising to 8.6 percent in April 2001 from 5.5 percent in

CHAPTER IV THE ROLE OF FINANCIAL DERIVATIVES IN EMERGING MARKETS

Table 9. Notional Amounts Outstanding of the Over-The-Counter and Exchange-Traded Derivatives
(In billions of U.S. dollars; end-June, 2001)

	Equity				Fixed Income				Foreign Exchange		
	Spot	Exchange-traded derivatives	OTC derivatives	Total derivatives in percent of the spot	Spot	Exchange-traded derivatives	OTC derivatives	Total derivatives in percent of the spot	Spot	Exchange-traded derivatives	OTC derivatives
Latin America											
Brazil	194.07	1.00	0.81	0.9	284.80	151.15	12.52	57.5	...	12.61	25.03
Mexico	154.91	0.01	...	0.0	82.30	4.58	...	5.6	...	0.10	...
Chile	44.31	...	0.00	0.0	34.00	...	0.10	0.3	...	...	5.86
Asia											
Singapore	197.62	6.80	0.38	3.6	48.30	459.96	32.00	1018.5	...	...	87.20
Hong Kong SAR	570.56	3.91	0.14	0.7	44.90	25.61	4.15	66.3	...	0.03	21.72
Korea	217.73	12.68	0.00	5.8	279.00	1.96	19.26	7.6	...	1.33	27.40
Taiwan Province of China	231.05	0.42	...	0.2	...	...	...	...	...	...	...
Malaysia	104.08	0.03	0.00	0.0	77.10	2.86	0.94	4.9	...	...	4.32
Europe, Middle East, and Africa											
South Africa	194.93	15.62	8.73	12.5	56.10	0.16	144.79	258.4	...	...	176.66
Hungary	9.34	0.05	0.00	0.6	17.20	0.06	0.09	0.9	...	0.17	0.28
Poland	25.56	0.04	0.00	0.2	37.60	...	0.85	2.3	...	0.01	7.36
Total	**1,944.16**	**40.56**	**10.07**	**2.6**	**961.30**	**646.33**	**214.69**	**89.6**	...	**14.24**	**355.82**
Memo item:											
Global Markets	29,843	1,905	2,039	13.2	29,710	17,493	75,813	314.1	...	66	20,435

Sources: BIS; IFC; MSCI; FOW TRADEdata; Exchanges; Bloomberg; and IMF staff estimates.

Notes: The notional amounts outstanding of the OTC traded derivatives are based on the data collected as part of the BIS 2001 Triennial Survey. All positions were reported on a worldwide consolidated basis (i.e., are based on global books of the head offices and all branches and subsidiaries of a given institutions), and only to the monetary authority of a country, where the parent institution had its head office.

The notional amounts outstanding of the exchange-traded derivatives are estimated using the data from the FOW TRADEdata, Bloomberg and various local exchanges. Notional amount is calculated as the number of contracts ("open interest" from FOW TRADEdata) multiplied by the face value of the contract in the U.S. dollar terms. In the case of index derivatives, the face value is the product of the contract's multiplier and the value of the underlying index. In the case of equity derivatives, individual stock futures and options are not included. The breakdown of exchange-traded derivatives by asset class (equity, fixed-income, currency) is based on the FOW TRADEdata classification, which, in some cases, differs from the BIS classification of the OTC derivatives. For example, the exchange-traded fixed income derivatives include a broader range of instruments than the single-currency interest rate swaps. In particular, in the case of Brazil, all cross currency swaps are included in the fixed-income derivatives category. For bond markets, the spot market capitalization is the total value of all outstanding domestic bonds based on the data provided by the BIS. The overall market capitalization of the global bond markets is the total value of all outstanding domestic bonds in all countries followed by the BIS. The overall market capitalization of the global equity markets is an estimated total market capitalization of all countries included in the MSCI All Country World Free Index. The equity market capitalization estimates for individual markets are based on the IFC data.

April 1998 (see Table 10). The declining trend in global currency markets was reversed during 2001–02, as the volume of euro/dollar contracts, which replaced the European legacy currency contracts, gradually increased and the volatility of G-3 currency pairs rose sharply in the first half of 2002. As a result, the total notional value of outstanding contracts in global OTC foreign exchange derivatives markets reached $18.5 trillion as of end-2002, approaching the mid-1998 level ($18.7 trillion).[63] Of note is the fact that the share of swaps in the total notional value of foreign exchange derivatives rose to 24 percent at the end of 2002 from 10 percent in mid-1998, which was generally attributed to a pickup in global syndicated loan and securities issuance.

In emerging markets, the most liquid OTC currency derivatives markets are in Singapore, Hong Kong SAR, and South Africa, where average daily turnover significantly exceeds the spot market turnover (see Table 10). Foreign exchange swaps and forwards are used by both foreign and domestic players for managing or gaining exposure to the exchange rate risk, with the trading volumes typically increasing during the times of large exchange rate movements. The buoyancy of

---

[63]Based on the BIS quarterly reports.

Table 10. Average Daily Turnover in the Over-The-Counter Derivatives Markets
(In billions of U.S. dollars)

	Total		Foreign Exchange		Interest Rate	
	April 1998	April 2001	April 1998	April 2001	April 1998	April 2001
Brazil	...	2.1	...	1.9	...	0.3
Chile	0.5	0.6	0.5	0.6	0	0
China	...	0	...	0	...	0
Czech Republic	3	1.4	3	1.2	0	0.2
Hong Kong SAR	51.4	52.0	48.9	49.4	2.4	2.6
Hungary	0.5	0.2	0.5	0.2	0	0
India	1.3	2	1.3	1.8	0	0.1
Indonesia	1	0.5	1	0.5	0	0
Korea	1.1	4	1	3.9	0	0.1
Malaysia	0.8	0.9	0.8	0.9	0	0
Mexico	2.6	4.6	2.4	4.2	0.2	0.4
Philippines	0.4	0.6	0.4	0.6	0	0
Poland	0.5	3.8	0.5	3.3	...	0.5
Russia	0.9	0.2	0.9	0.2	0	0
Singapore	90.7	72.5	85.4	69.3	5.3	3.2
South Africa	6	8.4	5.2	7.9	0.8	0.6
Taiwan Province of China	1.6	1.8	1.5	1.7	0.1	0.1
Thailand	2.2	1.3	2.2	1.3	0	0
Turkey	...	0.7	...	0.7	...	0
Total	**164.5**	**157.6**	**155.5**	**149.6**	**8.8**	**8.1**

Source: Bank for International Settlements, *Triennial Central Bank Survey 2001*.
Note: Turnover is defined as the absolute gross value of all new deals entered into during the month of April. No distinction is made between sales and purchases. The basis for reporting is the location of the office where any given deal was struck, so transactions concluded abroad were not reported by the country of location of the head office.

these markets tends to be affected by the stringency of local currency regulation and by the degree of foreign investor participation. In Singapore, a notable pickup in cross-currency swaps activity occurred after 1998, when the government allowed foreign entities to issue Singapore dollar bonds and to swap the proceeds into foreign currency for use outside the country. Furthermore, in 2002, the government removed the restriction that did not allow foreigners to engage in cross currency swap transactions unless there was an underlying economic activity. In Korea, up until 1999, the development of the onshore currency derivatives market was constrained by a legal requirement that any forward transaction had to be certified as a hedge against future current account flow (the so-called "real demand principle") and therefore, most of the won/dollar forward trades took place offshore. In South Africa, the turnover in foreign exchange swaps caught up with the spot market turnover around the time of the Asian crisis and significantly surpassed the latter in subsequent years (see Figure 15). However, the swaps market liquidity has deteriorated notably since late 2001, when the central bank stepped up the enforcement of currency regulation requiring market participants to provide evidence of an underlying trade flow for every forward or swap transaction, and, as a result, many foreigners pulled out of the South African foreign exchange market (see Figure 16).[64]

By contrast with Singapore, Hong Kong SAR, and South Africa, a significant share of currency derivatives trading in Brazil takes place at the organized exchange—Bolsa de Mercadorias & Futuros of São Paulo (BM&F).

---

[64]This restriction is similar to the Korean "real demand principle." It was aimed at limiting speculative activity, but was never strictly enforced until late 2001.

CHAPTER IV   THE ROLE OF FINANCIAL DERIVATIVES IN EMERGING MARKETS

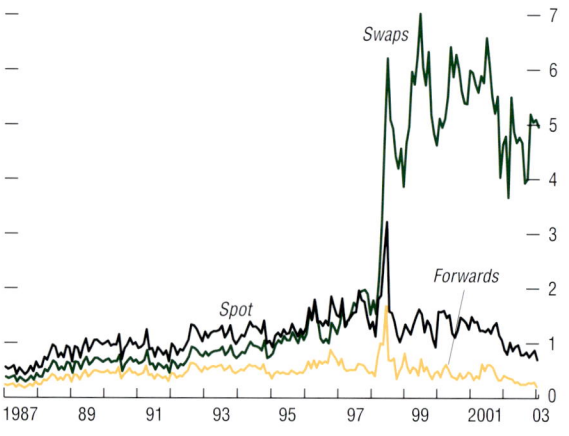

Figure 15. Average Daily Turnover in the South African Foreign-Exchange Market by Type of Transaction
(In billions of U.S. dollars)

Source: The South African Reserve Bank.

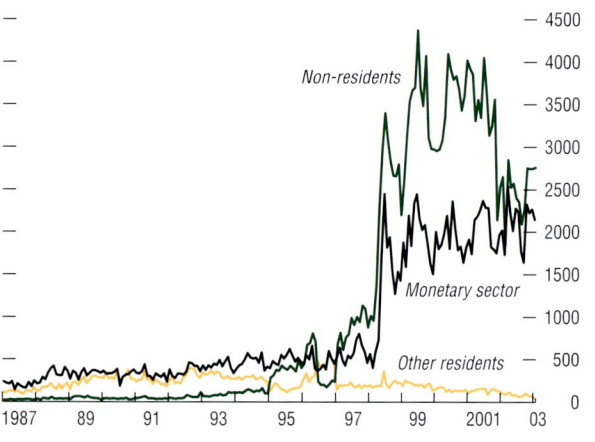

Figure 16. Average Daily Turnover in the South African Foreign-Exchange Swap Market
(In millions of U.S. dollars)

Source: The South African Reserve Bank.

Besides certain features of the country's legal framework that had hampered the development of the OTC market, the BM&F itself was actively trying to absorb part of the OTC business (see Box 7).[65] The expansion of currency derivatives in Brazil was stimulated by the flotation of the *real* in early 1999 and regulatory authorization for OTC derivatives on foreign exchange, interest rates, and price indexes. The change in the exchange rate regime coincided with sharply higher volatility in both the *real*/dollar rate and Brazilian interest rates, contributing to the creation of a "hedge culture." Most of the derivatives contracts are "nondeliverable" because historically, the BM&F did not want local derivatives markets to be limited either by less than free convertibility of the *real* or by the size of the spot market, with the latter also being susceptible to short squeezes. In contrast to the rapid growth of derivatives markets in Brazil, the development of exchange-traded derivatives in Mexico has been slower, primarily because the exchanges in Chicago (which are in the same time zone) have launched numerous derivative products based on Mexican underlying assets.

The "nondeliverable" forward (NDF) contracts tend to be the principal instruments in the offshore derivatives markets for many emerging market currencies and are often preferred by foreign investors who have restricted access to onshore markets and want to either avoid potential costs of delivering local currencies or reduce their counterparty credit risk exposure. In most cases, NDF markets trade at a premium to local markets because offshore financial institutions have limited access to local funding. In Taiwan Province of China, for example, the average implied one-year NDF yields were around 150

[65]For example, the uncertainty about the enforceability of close-out netting provisions in an insolvency scenario is often mentioned as one of the factors that hampered the development of the OTC market in Brazil.

Box 7. The Bolsa de Mercadorias & Futuros of São Paulo

The Bolsa de Mercadorias & Futuros (BM&F) of São Paulo, Brazil, which started operations in January 1986, ranks among the largest exchange-traded derivatives markets in the world in terms of the number of contracts transacted annually. In 2001, almost 98 million contracts were traded with a total open interest of 74 million contracts. These figures were surpassed in 2002: by the end of 2002 the cumulative number of contracts traded was 105.8 million. According to International Financial Services, London, the BM&F ranked ninth in terms of the number of contracts traded by the end of 2001, being surpassed among emerging markets only by the Korean Stock Exchange.

Trading at the BM&F takes place through the auction market system, which comprises both the exchange floor and the electronic trading system. Most contracts are traded in the auction market system, which accounted for 94 percent of all contracts traded and 97 percent of financial volume in 2001, while the over-the-counter (OTC) system accounted for the remaining transactions. The performance of all contracts traded through the auction system is guaranteed by the BM&F Derivatives Clearinghouse, which uses a safeguard structure based on intraday risk limits, market concentration limits, and collateral requirements imposed on clearing members, brokerage houses, and customers. The safeguard structure is complemented with three clearinghouse funds that provide additional levels of protection against counterparty risk. Other transactions in the OTC market system must be registered either with the BM&F or the Central of Custody and Financial Settlement (CETIP) if at least one of the counterparties is a financial institution. The settlement of OTC contracts registered with the BM&F can be guaranteed by the exchange upon request of the contractual parties provided the contract is written according to the BM&F specifications, which ensures a certain level of standardization. In practice, most of the OTC contracts are guaranteed by the BM&F.

The BM&F offers end users of the exchange a substantial number of contracts, allowing them to hedge risks or acquire market exposure. Futures contracts are available on a number of commodities, including gold, on the São Paulo Exchange Stock Index (Ibovespa); on foreign currencies, including the U.S. dollar and the euro; and on interest rates, including short and long interbank deposit rates, and the local U.S. dollar interest rate (Cupom Cambial). Option contracts are available on gold, interbank deposit rates, the Ibovespa, and the U.S. dollar. However, liquidity in the BM&F is heavily concentrated in a few contracts, including the one-day interbank deposit futures contracts or DI Futures, U.S. Dollar Futures, especially for those with maturities of one year or less, Ibovespa Index Futures, and Cupom Cambial Futures. Some of these contracts are described next.

DI Futures. This contract allows end users to hedge or take positions on local interest rate risk. The contract size is 1 million *reais* and the underlying asset is the capitalized daily interbank deposit rate, as measured by the Certificate of Deposit rate, verified on the period between the trading day and the business day preceding the expiration date of the contract, which is the first business day of the contract month. All contracts are settled on a cash basis. Contracts months include the first four months subsequent to the month during which a trade is made, and months that initiate a quarter (January, April, July, and October). DI Futures with maturities less than two years enjoy good liquidity, with an average daily turnover in the range of $5 billion to $10 billion.

Foreign exchange derivatives. The two- and three-month U.S. Dollar Futures, with contract sizes of $50,000, are the most traded and liquid contracts, with an average daily trading volume of around $3 billion. Contract months include every month of the year

Note: This box was prepared by Jorge Chan-Lau.

> **Box 7** *(concluded)*
>
> and should be settled on a cash basis the next business day following the last business day of the previous month. Hedging and speculation in the foreign exchange market can also be accomplished via U.S. Dollar European and American Options in the auction and OTC market systems, respectively. The average daily trading volume in this market is only around $250 million, a fraction of the volume traded in the futures market. In terms of open interest, though, U.S. Dollar Options accounted for 30 percent of total exchange-traded foreign currency instruments by the end of July 2002.
>
> *Ibovespa Index Futures.* Local investors can engage in index arbitrage and hedge positions on the main Brazilian stock market index, Ibovespa, through Ibovespa Index Futures. The contract size in Brazilian *reais* is equal to three times the level of the index. These contracts mature every two months and are settled on a cash basis on the next business day following the Wednesday closest to the 15th calendar day, which is the last trading day. Trading in the Ibovespa index futures comprises 86 percent of total trading in stock index instruments, as measured by number of traded contracts.
>
> *Cupom Cambial Futures.* The Cupom Cambial for a given maturity is the spread between the local interest rate, as measured by the interest rate on interbank deposits, and the exchange rate variation during the life of the contract. From this definition, it is clear that the Cupom Cambial is equivalent to the onshore U.S. dollar interest rate and, hence, its level is affected by corporate demand for foreign currency hedging. The Cupom Cambial Futures allow local market participants—mostly nonfinancial companies, banks, and mutual funds—to position themselves in the local U.S. dollar interest rate market. Contract size is $50,000 and contract months and expiration dates are established by the BM&F. Contracts are settled in cash.
>
> The BM&F follows state-of-the-art risk management procedures to deal with market risk, liquidity risk, and counterparty risk. These procedures have helped the BM&F to withstand several episodes of market turbulence, including the January 1999 crisis, the Argentina crisis by the end of 2001, and the current volatility associated to the recent presidential elections. Despite this impressive track record, the BM&F remains highly exposed to sovereign risk, as close to 90 percent of the exchange's collateral is comprised by Federal Government Bonds.

basis points higher than onshore rates during 2001–02. In Korea, the existence of the "real demand principle" spurred the development of a liquid offshore NDF market in the Korean won. However, after this restriction was lifted in 1999, a lot of activity moved onshore, leading to the convergence of the offshore and onshore prices. In some cases, however, offshore markets continue to perform functions that are not performed by onshore markets. For example, while both onshore and offshore forward markets in Korea are most liquid in maturities of up to one year, the NDFs and swaps can be structured in tenors of up to 10 years in the offshore market.

Compared with other emerging markets, the liquidity in the Central European onshore derivatives markets remains limited due to the lack of effective infrastructure and also to some extent existing regulatory constraints on the use of hedging instruments by local corporates and pension funds. Hungary has seen a strong pickup in currency derivatives trading since the move to greater exchange rate flexibility and removal of capital controls; but, compared with Poland, liquidity is still low (see Tables 9 and 10). Many of the derivatives linked to the Central European currencies are reportedly traded offshore, mainly out of London. More recently, both Poland and Hungary have made significant progress in improving legal and documentation infrastructure for derivatives trading. The Polish government adopted new provisions on netting and credit support, while in Hungary, the close-out netting provisions came into effect in January 2002. Legal certainty regarding enforceability of close-out netting reduces credit risk arising from OTC derivatives transactions by allowing market participants to calculate their net obligation vis-à-vis an insolvent party.

Fixed-Income Derivatives

In contrast to recent trends in global currency derivatives market, the global fixed-income derivatives market continued to expand steadily over the past few years, with interest rate swaps (IRS) being the largest and the fastest growing market segment. From end-1998 to end-2002, the notional value of all outstanding interest rate contracts in the global OTC market doubled, reaching $102 trillion (see BIS, 2002b). The rapid expansion of the IRS activity was triggered by the liquidity crunch in the spot and exchange-traded derivatives markets during the Russia/LTCM crisis and the reduction in the U.S. government bond market liquidity due to the planned debt repayments. These were generally seen as the main factors that forced market participants to look for alternative hedging and benchmark instruments and encouraged the shift into the OTC swap market (see IMF, 2001). Following the collapse of the telecommunications, media, and technology (TMT) bubble, an increased equity price volatility and a continued decline in interest rates forced many investors, including those in emerging markets, to shift from stocks to bonds, turning to the bond futures and IRS markets either in search of yield or to hedge their bond exposures. The structure of the global fixed-income derivatives market is similar to that of currency derivatives—that is, the OTC segment is significantly larger (when measured in terms of notional values) than the exchange segment, although the average daily turnover in the latter is higher, possibly due to shorter maturity of the exchange-traded instruments.

In emerging market countries, the most liquid fixed-income derivatives markets are in Singapore, Hong Kong SAR, Brazil, Mexico, and South Africa (see Tables 9–11). In Latin America and Singapore, most of the fixed-income derivatives trading takes place at the organized exchanges, but in Korea and South

Table 11. Exchange-Traded Options and Futures Contract Trading Volume, 2002

	Stock	Equity Index	Government Debt	Interest Rate	Foreign Exchange
Latin America					
Brazil	89,740,269	6,979,515	15,230	51,116,740	18,179,225
Mexico	...	49,243	3,579,165	80,606,463	52,108
Asia					
Singapore	13,690	10,458,364	699,448	21,714,364	...
Hong Kong SAR	3,745,816	6,995,635	3,673	281,227	3,503
Korea	57,918	1,933,072,470	12,802,781	3,788	1,436,191
Taiwan Province of China	...	7,944,254	...	...	...
Malaysia	...	233,864	80,419	64,307	...
EMEA					
South Africa	10,326,227	19,018,736	32,765	...	...
Hungary	365,150	282,973	...	...	...
Poland	92,097	3,322,855	...	...	5,957

Source: International Federation of Stock Exchanges (FIBV)

CHAPTER IV THE ROLE OF FINANCIAL DERIVATIVES IN EMERGING MARKETS

Africa it is mainly concentrated in the OTC market (see Table 9). Those markets that were deregulated more extensively (most notably in Korea) experienced the fastest growth. In terms of notional values, the Singapore Exchange (SGX) is still far ahead of other emerging markets, with most traded fixed-income derivative contracts including Euroyen LIBOR, Euroyen TIBOR, and Eurodollar futures and options. The rapid pickup in the fixed-income derivatives activity in Mexico was due to an increased government bond issuance, easier access to derivatives trading for local banks and brokers (because of a relaxation of certain administrative restrictions), and the introduction of new products by the Mexican Derivatives Exchange (MexDer) (see Figure 17). In contrast to Mexico, the fixed-income derivatives activity in Brazil has contracted, largely reflecting the weakness of the underlying bond market.

Falling interest rates and increased local bond issuance were the main factors that spurred the expansion of the local currency IRS markets. In addition, the proliferation of structured products in Hong Kong SAR, Korea, and, more recently, Taiwan Province of China created additional demand for instruments, such as interest rate swaps, which are used to hedge these exposures. In some countries, most notably in Brazil and Hong Kong SAR, the IRS market has become more liquid than the underlying cash market and as a result performs functions that are typically provided by bond markets, such as price discovery and provision of benchmarks. For example, in Brazil, the local swap curve is the benchmark yield curve for maturities beyond one year. In Hong Kong SAR, given the relatively small size of Exchange Fund bond issues, the swap market is more liquid and therefore drives the pricing of local bonds. By contrast, the South African government bond yield curve remains the benchmark curve, despite the fact that the outstanding notional value of local currency interest rate swaps significantly exceeds the local bond market capi-

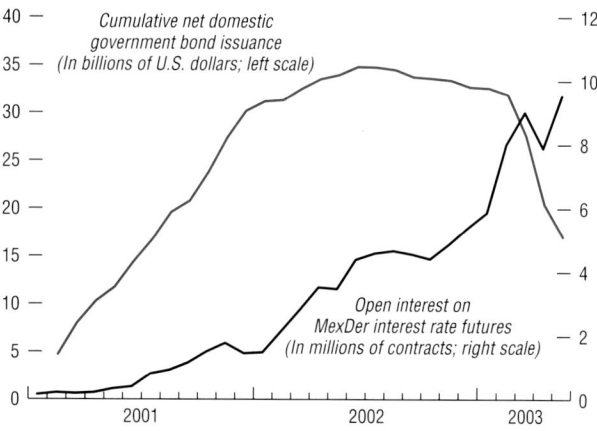

Figure 17. Mexican Bond Issuance and Interest Rate Futures

Sources: Dealogic; MexDer; and IMF staff estimates.

talization. This is largely due to the fact that the South African government's debt management policy was specifically aimed at maintaining and improving the liquidity of the benchmark bond issues.

In some countries, the presence of sophisticated institutional investors and the relaxation of restrictions on their participation in local derivatives markets contributed to the rapid expansion of the fixed-income derivatives activity. For instance, one of the key drivers behind the growth of the IRS market in Korea was the entry of the investment trust companies that were allowed to hedge up to 5 percent of total assets using local derivatives. In Singapore, insurance companies, which form the core of the local institutional investor base, increased their participation in the longer-dated interest rate derivatives market as well. Similarly, in Taiwan Province of China, pension and insurance companies became more active users of debt-related derivatives, following their shift toward fixed-income investments and away from equity and real estate. In South Africa, unit trusts are less involved in the swap market because of a number of restrictions. However, other institutional investors are very active in the IRS market, with local banks concentrating on the one- to five-year maturity segment and pension funds—on the 5+ year spectrum. In Mexico, the regulatory authorities have recently issued guidelines for pension funds limiting their use of derivative products only by a certain level of the Value-at-Risk measure. Because in many countries regulation allows local institutional investors to use only standardized exchange-traded products, the introduction or, in some cases, widening of the range of such instruments may be a necessary condition for further expansion of the derivatives activity.[66]

In contrast to the IRS markets, the government bond futures markets in emerging economies tend to be less active. Since bond futures are primarily used for hedging the underlying bond exposures, the liquidity in bond futures is very sensitive to the spot market activity. For instance, the average trading volume of the three-year Korean government bond future contract has closely mirrored the performance of the underlying bond since the introduction of the derivative contract in September 1999 (see Figure 18). Thus, countries with less developed government bond markets are generally less successful in developing bond futures markets, especially when there are alternative hedging instruments that are sufficiently liquid. One example is the future contract on the five-year Singapore government bond, which was launched in June 2001 but never took off in earnest, with the average daily volume falling from 878 contracts in July 2001 to only about 10 contracts at the end of 2002. This was partly due to the weak activity in the underlying instrument, but also to the fact that local banks, which were the main holders of government bonds, could hedge their bond positions more efficiently by using swaps. South Africa is another interesting case, where the bond market is very liquid and there are several benchmark bond futures listed on the exchange; however, most of them are rarely traded. The illiquidity of bond futures in South Africa is explained by the existence of a very liquid domestic bond repo market (the so-called "carry market").

Equity Derivatives

Compared to currency and fixed-income derivatives, the equity-based derivative products represent a much smaller part of the

---

[66]While in the OTC market, the derivative product is guaranteed by the issuer, the contracts listed on an exchange are guaranteed by the exchange. Thus, in the latter case, the counterparty risk is typically lower. Other advantages of using standardized derivative products offered by organized exchanges include faster execution, easier liquidation of contracts, and lower transaction costs.

CHAPTER IV THE ROLE OF FINANCIAL DERIVATIVES IN EMERGING MARKETS

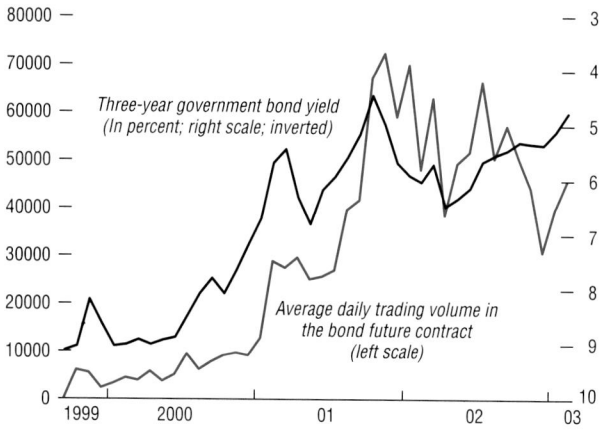

Figure 18. Korean Government Bond Futures

Sources: Bloomberg L.P.; and FOW TRADE data.

global market, with the bulk of activity concentrated at the organized exchanges. This reflects in part the diminishing role of local equity markets as a source of funding for local entities. Nonetheless, the volume of exchange-traded equity futures and options in most major markets rose steadily over the past few years, as the increased volatility in global equity markets, as well as the introduction of retail-oriented and sector-based products, led more market participants to use equity derivatives.

While most exchanges in emerging Asia experienced steady expansion in equity derivative products over recent years, the stock index derivatives' growth in Korea was spectacular (see Figure 19). The average daily trading volume in KOSPI 200 options and futures, which are the most liquid derivative contracts traded on the Korean Stock Exchange (KSE), rose to 4.7 million contracts at the end of 2002 from 0.9 million contracts at the end of 2000.[67] As a result, Korea now accounts for about 30 percent of global turnover in stock index derivatives.[68] The average daily volume of index futures and options traded on Taiwan Futures Exchange (Taifex) doubled between the end of 2000 and the end of 2002. Outside Asia, South Africa has the most developed equity derivatives market in the emerging markets universe. In fact, the outstanding notional of equity derivative products traded on the Johannesburg Stock Exchange (JSE) and the South African Futures Exchange (SAFEX)

---

[67]The increase in the average daily trading volume of the KOSPI 200 options was even more stunning—from 1.6 million contracts in December 2000 to 9 million contracts in December 2002 (all contract volumes are based on the information provided by the FOW TRADEdata).

[68]Given that equity index derivative contracts traded on KSE are of a significantly smaller size than those traded on major exchanges, KSE is not considered in the BIS global ranking of exchanges. However, according to the BIS quarterly survey, KSE is the largest derivatives exchange in the world based on the number of contracts traded.

exceeded that of the KSE in mid-2001 (see Table 9). However, the derivatives trading volumes on JSE/SAFEX declined during the past few years, reflecting the trends in the underlying equity market, the ongoing consolidation in the banking sector and asset management industry, and the retrenchment of some foreign liquidity providers. In Latin America, the average daily trading volume of stock index derivatives at the Brazilian Bovespa is the highest in the region and is roughly similar to that of South Africa and most markets in emerging Asia (excluding Korea).

The individual stock options traded in emerging markets are typically significantly less liquid than benchmark index futures and options. Although the cross-country comparisons of the outstanding notional values of single equity derivatives in emerging markets are hampered by data availability, based on the number of contracts traded, Bovespa appears to be by far the most active market for single equity derivatives in the emerging markets universe (see Table 11). In South Africa, single stock options exist for about 40 corporate names, but are significantly less liquid than index options. These instruments are typically launched in the OTC market and subsequently listed on the exchange.

Local equity derivatives in emerging markets are used by a wide range of market participants. Local corporates are the main users of single stock options. Asset managers, who are typically benchmarked against various indices, are the main users of stock index futures and options, while pension funds often prefer equity-linked notes. Market data for Korea indicates that domestic individual investors tend to be the most active users of stock index futures traded on local exchanges (see Figure 20). Similarly, around 90 percent of the futures market in Taiwan is reportedly represented by retail investors. In South Africa, both residents and nonresidents participate in the market, with foreigners at times accounting for half of the trading volume. However, in contrast with Asian markets, the retail

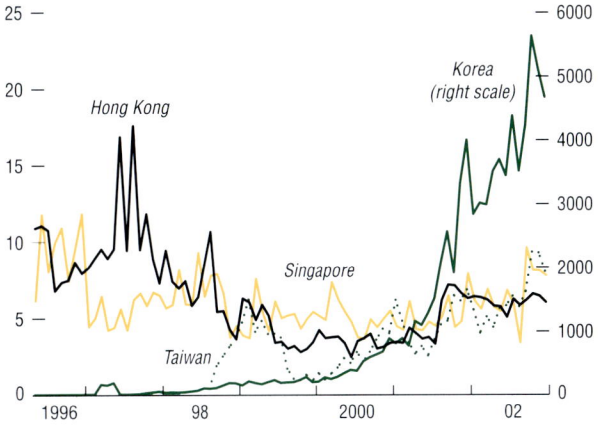

Figure 19. Average Daily Trading Volumes in Equity Index Derivatives in Asia
(In thousands of contracts)

Source: FOW TRADE data.

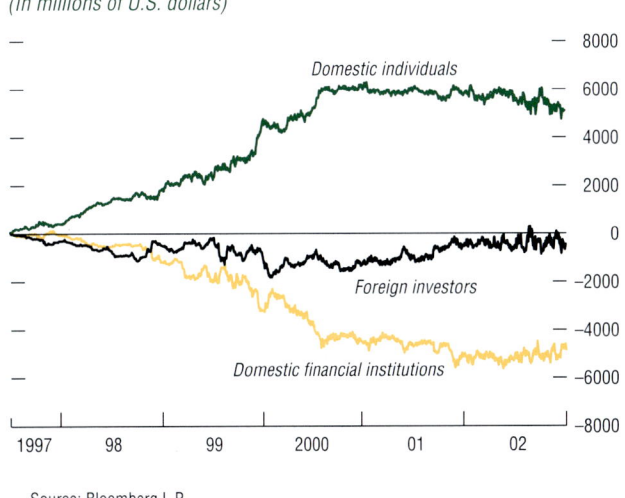

Figure 20. KOSPI 200 Index Futures: Cumulative Net Purchases
(In millions of U.S. dollars)

Source: Bloomberg L.P.

investor base for equity derivatives in South Africa is fairly small.

Over the past two years, many derivatives exchanges around the world took measures to increase individual investor participation. Both the Hong Kong Exchanges and Clearing (HKE) and the Taiwan Futures Exchange (Taifex) introduced new products targeting individual investors, such as small-sized equity index futures and also the so-called equity-linked principal protected products.[69] According to market sources, the equity-linked principal protected products market in Hong Kong SAR reached more than $1.5 billion in late 2002. Similar instruments are expected to rapidly gain popularity in Korea, where the retail investor base is larger than in Hong Kong SAR. However, more recently, some KSE officials began to voice concerns over excessively high individual investor participation in the futures market, saying that retail investors could exacerbate volatility by following the investment patterns of the better-informed foreign institutional investors. Outside Asia, many emerging market exchanges took steps to increase individual investor participation as well. For example, the Brazilian Bovespa launched the small-sized equity index contracts in September 2001.

Credit Derivatives

Although the credit derivatives market is still a small part of the global derivatives market, it remains one of the fastest-growing segments notwithstanding several major credit events that occurred during the past few years (Russia, Argentina, and Enron). The data collected as part of the BIS Triennial Survey showed that positions in the global credit derivatives market rose to $693 billion at the end of June 2001 from $118 billion at the end of June 1998. Separately, according to the British Bankers' Association (BBA) Credit Derivatives Report 2001/2002 (see Deutsche Bank, 2003), the total notional value of all credit derivatives products referencing both mature and emerging market names stood at $1,189 billion as of end-2001.

The emerging credit derivatives market mainly consists of credit protection instruments on external sovereign bonds that are traded offshore. The estimates of the size of this market range from $40 billion for the outstanding notional as of mid-2001, according to a *Risk* survey, to $300 billion suggested by Deutsche Bank.[70] Nonetheless, this means that the share of emerging market instruments in the global credit derivatives market is much larger than their share in other global derivatives markets. The most commonly used credit derivatives in emerging markets are credit default swaps (CDSs), credit-linked notes (CLNs), and collateralized debt obligations (CDOs).[71] The sovereign CDSs are the most liquid instruments in the emerging credit derivatives market, accounting for around 85 percent of the total outstanding notional. The most actively traded contracts reference the external sovereign bonds issued by Korea,

---

[69]These instruments typically provide for a minimum principal amount to be repaid to investors and a variable return amount based on the performance of an index or a portfolio of securities.

[70]Both estimates exclude emerging Asia. Deutsche Bank is believed to be the largest broker-dealer in the emerging market credit derivatives.

[71]A *credit default swap* is a financial contract under which the protection buyer pays a periodic fee (expressed in basis points per notional) in return for a payment by the protection seller contingent on the occurrence of a credit event. A *credit-linked note* is a security with principal and/or coupon payments linked to the occurrence of a credit event with respect to reference entity (i.e., it is a structured note with an embedded default swap). In a synthetic *collateralized debt obligation* (CDO), the issuer of notes (protection buyer) is typically either a special purpose vehicle or a bank and the payments are usually linked to a portfolio (which may be actively managed) of default swaps referencing a variety of credit risks. The proceeds from issuance of CDOs are reinvested in a collateral consisting of highly rated government securities, which is used to pay interest and principal on the notes.

Mexico, Brazil, Russia, and Singapore.[72] A relatively few top-tier corporate credits (in Latin America, these include mainly Mexican names, such as Telmex and Cemex) are also traded in the CDS market, but these instruments are considerably less liquid and reportedly account for less than 5 percent of the emerging CDS market/ex-Asia. Compared with other regions, the CDS activity in emerging Asia has been limited by the relatively small size of the external sovereign bond market. However, the CDSs are rapidly gaining popularity, as they often provide higher market liquidity, higher returns, and longer yield curves than the U.S. dollar-denominated sovereign bonds. According to market sources, the average daily trading volume in the Asian CDS market rose to $200 million in 2002 from $100–150 million in 2001. Also, several investment banks have recently launched credit derivative index (CDI) products that allow investors to gain exposure to portfolios of credit-default swaps referencing sovereign or corporate names in emerging markets.[73]

Market participants use credit default swaps for hedging against (or gaining exposure to) changes in credit spreads and default risk. Compared with bonds, the CDSs have several advantages: (1) credit default swaps allow positions in maturities for which the cash instruments are illiquid or unavailable; (2) there is typically no collateral or up-front cash payment; and (3) the credit default swaps provide investors with an opportunity to take a short position vis-à-vis a particular credit for a longer term than in the repo market, in which positions typically have to be rolled over every one-to-three months.[74] In fact, emerging market credit default swaps are often used to take exposure to sovereigns for maturities shorter than those corresponding to outstanding bonds and to express views on sovereign default risk and on cross-country relative values (see Box 8).

Some emerging markets over the past few years experienced a pickup in local credit derivatives activity. In Brazil, the government has made the first steps toward developing the onshore credit derivatives markets by allowing local banks to trade credit risk. Also, the Brazilian Central Bank issued a circular outlining the accounting procedures for credit derivatives in 2001, and the Brazilian payment and settlement system for OTC markets (CETIP) launched a registration system for credit default swaps in early 2004. In Korea, there has been a notable pickup in local currency credit-linked notes referencing Korean corporate, sovereign, and quasi-sovereign credits. According to the Bank of Korea, the volume of CLNs rose to $1.2 billion in 2002 from $0.7 billion in 2001. The main attractions of CLNs for Korean investors are higher yield and longer duration compared with those offered by government and corporate bonds. In South Africa, credit derivatives activity picked up in 2000–01 amid low interest rates on government bonds, but stalled after the central bank hiked the rates. According to market sources, the credit default swaps of up to one-year maturity currently exist for only a few South African corporates. In general, the expansion of credit derivatives in emerging markets is constrained by the relatively small

---

[72]This is based on the emerging markets credit derivatives survey conducted by the Emerging Markets Trading Association (EMTA) and released in May 2003. The questionnaire requested notional values of all credit derivatives traded during the period from January 1 to March 31, 2003. A total of 22 internationally active banks participated in the survey (excluding Deutsche Bank).

[73]For example, J.P. Morgan has recently launched the Emerging Markets Derivative Index (EMDI), which is a basket of 19 sovereign CDSs. Separately, Merrill Lynch has launched the Asia-Liquid Indexed Credits (Asia-LINC), with 25 reference entities in the basket representing corporate credits from China, Hong Kong SAR, India, Korea, Malaysia, Philippines, Singapore, Taiwan Province of China, and Thailand.

[74]An obvious disadvantage is that as with any insurance contract, no payout occurs if protection expires before the credit event.

Box 8. Credit Default Swap Spreads in Emerging Markets

The credit default swap curve, a plot of credit default swap spreads for different maturities, conveys useful information about market views on a sovereign's ability to honor its external debt, as well as the recovery value bond investors can obtain in case of debt default. The credit default swap curve is normally upward sloping because credit deterioration is more likely in the medium and long term than in the short term. If the sovereign is able to meet its debt repayments in the short term, changes in market perception about debt sustainability would likely result into parallel or steepening movements of the credit default swap curve. In contrast, problems associated to short-term financing needs would lead to a flattening of the credit default swap curve, as short-term spreads widen to compensate protection sellers for the increase in short-term risk. During periods of market stress, the credit default swap curve can become inverted, as in the case of Argentina during the second half of 2001, and more recently, of Brazil since June 2002.

Further information on default probabilities for a sovereign for different time horizons can be extracted using standard credit default swap valuation models. The Figure shows the evolution of one-year and two-year default probabilities for Argentina between January 1990 and December 2001.[1] The approval of an IMF package for Argentina at the end of 2000 contributed to soothe investors' sentiment and reversed a sharp spike in default probabilities experienced in November 2000. However, increased concerns

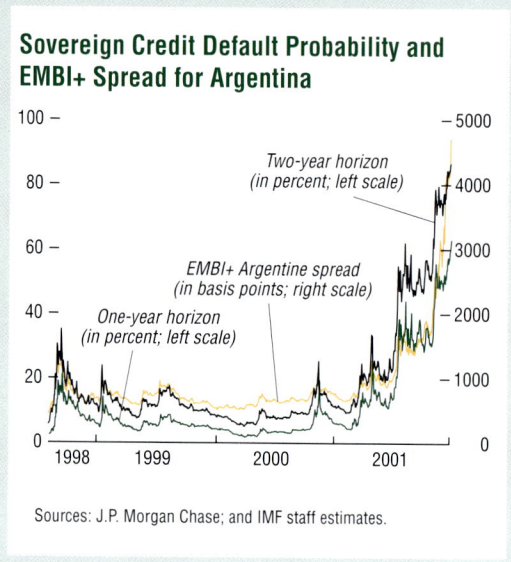

Sources: J.P. Morgan Chase; and IMF staff estimates.

about the ability of Argentina to meet its debt payments amid continued deterioration of the country's fiscal position, together with an uncertain political climate, caused default probabilities to creep upwards during 2001. By the end of the second half of 2001, default probabilities reached levels not observed ever before. As it became clear that no further external aid was forthcoming and that the government would refrain from implementing significant fiscal measures, default probabilities increased significantly at the end of the third quarter of 2001. By mid-December 2001, trading on Argentina default swaps stopped completely as no participant was willing to take a long position on Argentina credit risk, a position validated by Argentina's default in January 2002.

Credit default swaps are not the only financial instruments that contain useful information about sovereign risk, as sovereign bond spreads are also useful indicators of sovereign debt solvency. Indeed, the Figure shows the

---

[1]Default probabilities were estimated using the credit derivatives pricing model described in Duffie (1999), and assuming a 25 percent recovery rate in case of default.

Note: This box was prepared by Jorge Chan-Lau.

> high correlation between the default probabilities implied by credit default swaps and the EMBI+ spread for Argentina.² However,
>
> ²A detailed analysis of different sovereign risk measures for emerging markets including implied default probabilities from credit default swaps and sovereign bond yields is provided in Chan-Lau and Sy (forthcoming).
>
> liquidity in the cash market is more likely to dry out during periods of stress than in the credit default swap markets. In fact, there is anecdotal evidence that following the serious disruptions in the cash market clearing mechanisms in the aftermath of the events of September 11, 2001, price discovery migrated from the cash market to the credit derivatives market.

size and illiquidity of the local corporate bond markets as well as by the lack of standardized documentation and regulatory uncertainties regarding the treatment of credit derivatives for accounting and tax purposes.[75] Nevertheless, local banks manage to get around these problems by offering CLNs, which reference corporate bonds and promissory notes that are unlisted but traded over-the-counter. Going forward, many market analysts foresee the local credit derivatives market providing price discovery for the spot market and, thus, encouraging securitization.

Local Derivatives Markets and Capital Flows to Emerging Economies

There is a broad consensus that the rapid expansion of derivatives products during the past 10 to 15 years was one of the key factors that facilitated the rise of global cross-border capital flows (see, for example, Garber, 1998; and Dodd, 2001). Various traditional cross-border investment vehicles, such as loans, bonds, equities, and FDI, can potentially expose both lenders and borrowers to foreign exchange risk, interest rate, market, credit, and refinancing (liquidity) risks. By allowing market participants to unbundle and redistribute these risks to those who are in a better position to manage them, derivatives make cross-border investments more attractive, thereby increasing net flows and creating more opportunities for portfolio diversification. There are many ways in which the use of derivatives by local and foreign market participants can facilitate cross-border capital flows. Here are a few examples.

Currency derivatives can be used to change the currency of denomination of asset holdings and, therefore, to hedge investments against unexpected changes in exchange rates by both foreign and local investors. Foreign investors typically use currency derivatives to hedge their long local currency exposure in emerging markets, while local entities often use the same instruments to manage foreign exchange risk associated with external financing, typically in G-3 currencies. Thus, the level of external fund-raising by local entities is directly related to the availability of the currency hedging instruments.

Another example is the basic single-currency interest-rate swap, which can allow the borrower with a floating interest rate loan/bond to hedge the interest rate risk by swapping floating rate payments for fixed-rate payments. Because interest rate swaps give

---

[75]The existence of a liquid corporate bond market is critical because the CDS counterparties use the underlying bond market to hedge their swap positions. In addition, the type of reference obligations most commonly included in a CDS contract is "bonds," and less often "bonds and loans" or "specified obligations."

borrowers an opportunity to exploit their comparative advantages for borrowing at fixed versus floating rates in different markets, they may encourage corporates or banks to seek external financing at more favorable terms instead of borrowing locally. Thus, the use of single-currency swaps can generate gross cross-border flows. In some emerging markets, most notably in Brazil, where the local corporate treasurers' benchmark is a floating local currency interest rate, whereas funds raised internationally are typically at a fixed U.S. dollar rate, interest rate swaps have become central to the ability of local entities to manage the risks associated with foreign borrowing.

Finally, credit derivatives represent another class of instruments that can potentially increase net flows into emerging markets. An attractive feature of credit derivatives is that they allow investors/lenders to manage the default/bankruptcy risks without having to buy or sell the underlying securities. For example, a foreign bank can reduce its credit exposure to a particular client without physically removing assets from its balance sheet and thus effectively separate relationship management from risk management. Some market analysts argue that if international banks could use onshore credit derivatives in emerging markets, they would be more willing to maintain or increase their exposure to local corporate clients.

Local Participation

Local entities with foreign exchange exposures are typically among the most active users of derivatives in emerging markets. Given that domestic financial markets in many emerging economies are not deep enough for large local corporates to borrow long term and in large size, domestic companies often have to rely on international bond or syndicated loan markets for this type of funding. Thus, when the local corporate sector has a positive net external financing requirement, the development of the onshore derivatives markets becomes a critical factor in facilitating external fund-raising. Of course, in the case when emerging market companies with the internationally diversified production (for example, the South African mining companies) limit their foreign currency borrowing strictly to financing those operations that earn income in the same currency, there may not be much need for foreign currency hedging. However, this financing decision may not necessarily be optimal, given the relative costs of funds (domestic versus external), and may be due to either the unavailability or the high cost of hedging instruments. The latter should be improving as the emerging derivatives markets become more mature.

The relative importance of derivatives for local entities' fund-raising in international markets varies across emerging economies. In Emerging Europe and Asia, this link is not as strong as in Latin America. Following the Asian crisis, many countries in emerging Asia shifted toward relying more on local currency financing. In addition, many of these countries are running current account surpluses and thus do not have positive net external financing requirements. In emerging Europe, local entities are still constrained by regulatory restrictions on the use of derivatives. By contrast, in Brazil, the link between fund-raising in international markets and derivatives activity has been particularly strong (see Figure 21). Virtually all local companies that have access to international financial markets raise U.S. dollar-denominated funds and then turn to the local derivatives market to swap the external financing obligations into *reais* with an interest rate indexed to the overnight (CDI) rate. Historically, the cost of U.S. dollar hedges in Brazil was fairly high due to the shortage of hedging instruments, as most domestic institutional investors did not have foreign currency positions (in contrast to the Chilean pension funds) and many exporters with the U.S. dollar receivables typically had overall net short U.S. dollar positions. As a result, Brazilian corporates tended to invest part of their cash reserves in U.S. dollar-denominated securities in order to provide at least partial protection against an adverse exchange rate move. In 1999, the Brazilian Central Bank (BCB) stepped in as the main provider of currency hedge to the market through the issuance of U.S. dollar linked securities. Furthermore, in March 2002, the BCB decided to split the exchange rate linked instruments into *real*-denominated bonds and foreign exchange swaps in order to lower its debt rollover costs and also to reduce the cost of currency hedging for local entities.[76]

The development of the domestic credit derivatives markets in emerging economies can facilitate a more accurate pricing of corporate credit risk and help to attract foreign capital flows going forward. Many analysts believe that since local market participants are more familiar with local credit risk and less concerned about market liquidity than foreign investors, they are "natural" sellers of credit protection on emerging market corporate risk. At the same time, the domestic financial institutions that already have exposure to local corporate credit risk (in the form of bonds, loans, and receivables) are in a better position to structure products that match local investors' preferences for credit risk than foreign banks. Thus, local market participants can play a key role in the development of the domestic market for corporate credit risk pro-

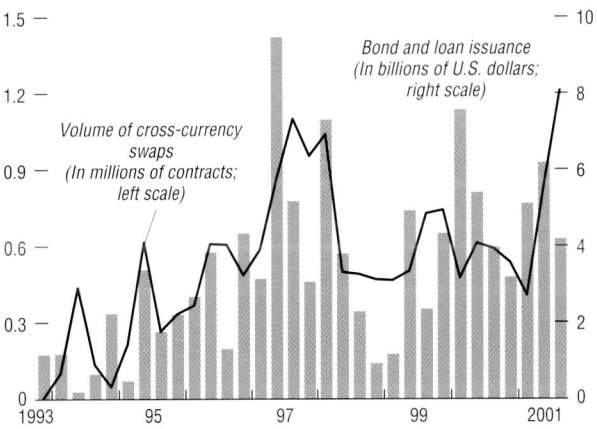

Figure 21. International Bond and Loan Issuance and Derivatives Trading Volume in Brazil

Sources: Dealogic; and FOW TRADE data.

---

[76]This move was intended to result in a more efficient pricing of both instruments and a reduction of the transaction costs for end users of these instruments, with mutual funds being the main users of the *real*-denominated bonds, and with local corporates being the main users of currency hedges. Before March 2002, Brazilian corporates had to pay a premium to the financial intermediaries for transferring the U.S. dollar hedge component of the U.S. dollar-linked bond to them through currency swap arrangements. Of course, the fact that the BCB became the main supplier of currency hedge to corporates did not remove the currency risk, but rather shifted the risk to the BCB. The question of how the BCB should manage this risk without adverse implications for exchange rate or macroeconomic stability is beyond the scope of this chapter.

tection. Of note is the fact that local institutional investors, particularly pension funds and insurance companies, have been gradually increasing their use of CLNs and structured products.

Foreign Participation

Foreign investors in emerging markets generally include banks, corporates, "real money" accounts (both dedicated and cross-over investment funds), and speculative money accounts (hedge funds and proprietary trading desks of investment and commercial banks). Compared with local entities, the foreign investors' participation in the emerging derivatives markets is fairly limited. Mexico, Hungary, Poland, and the Czech Republic have seen a considerable demand by international investors for long-term interest rate and local currency exposures that was driven in part by the so-called "convergence trades," with exposures established in both cash and derivatives markets.[77] As far as the OTC markets are concerned, the extent of foreign investor participation (both as final users of the derivative products as well as intermediaries) varies. In some countries, such as Singapore, Hong Kong SAR, and South Africa, foreign dealers account for the bulk of the turnover in the OTC markets, while in other countries, most of the trading goes through domestic dealers.

Both anecdotal evidence and industry surveys suggest that "real money" funds hedge relatively little of their risk exposures in emerging markets, either because of internal restrictions on leveraged positions or because these risk exposures are desirable. A survey of derivatives usage by U.S. institutional investors conducted by the NYU Stern School of Business in 1998 (Hayt and Levich, 1999) showed that only 46 percent of respondents were permitted to use derivatives by their investment mandate, and only 27 percent of respondents had open derivatives positions at the time of the survey. Because many emerging market countries maintain various restrictions on foreign participation in local derivatives markets, one would expect that the percentage of the emerging market funds using local derivatives to hedge various risk exposures is even lower.

Even when there are no restrictions on foreign participation in emerging derivatives markets, foreign investors (equity investors, in particular) often prefer to take outright foreign currency exposure. Thus, one would not expect to find a strong link between foreign inflows and derivatives activity even in those emerging markets, where foreign participation is significant. Indeed, our analysis of foreign institutional investors' purchases of stocks in Brazil, Korea, Taiwan Province of China, and South Africa and the trading volumes in the onshore currency and equity derivatives markets suggests that there is no statistically significant relationship between foreign purchases of shares and derivatives' trading volumes in these countries.[78] It should be noted that in some emerging markets, local equities are a "natural hedge" against the foreign exchange risk (for example, in South Africa, the share prices of mining companies with dollar receivables are often referred to as "rand hedges"). Unlike equity investors, bond investors sometimes do hedge their long local-currency bond exposures in emerging markets. Also, in those emerging markets where bond repo markets are sufficiently liquid, foreign investors often prefer to repo bonds instead of purchasing bonds outright and

---

[77]The term "convergence trade" refers to a bet that the local inflation rate (and thus long-term interest rates) in an emerging market will converge to a particular developed market rate (in the United States or in the EU) within a certain period of time or as economic integration progresses.

[78]This exercise uses monthly time series of foreign purchases of local shares (from Bloomberg) and trading volumes in local equity and foreign exchange derivatives markets (from the FOW TRADEdata).

simultaneously hedging the foreign exchange risk with derivatives.

In contrast with the "real money" accounts, speculative investors can use derivatives freely for hedging risks associated with their cash market positions or for gaining leveraged returns or for exploiting relative value opportunities between the cash and derivatives markets. However, according to Credit Suisse First Boston/Tremont, the leading provider of the hedge fund indices, the hedge funds that invest in emerging markets often employ a long-only strategy because "many emerging markets do not allow short selling, nor offer viable futures or other derivative products with which to hedge."[79] In contrast to many other emerging markets, foreigners were the dominant players in the South African foreign exchange and interest rate swap markets until late 2001 (see Figure 16), using derivatives either to bet on their currency and interest rate views or to proxy-hedge the emerging market risk (with the latter due to the rand being one of the most liquid currencies in the emerging markets universe).

Both leveraged investors and dedicated emerging market debt funds are active participants in the credit derivatives markets for emerging market U.S. dollar-denominated bonds. The main protection sellers in credit derivatives markets are the major internationally active banks. Hedge funds have been active users of emerging market credit derivatives, mainly focusing on trading the basis between default swaps and bonds amid increased volatility in emerging debt markets.[80] The "convertible arbitrage" funds have also been among the active buyers of credit protection, using credit default swaps to strip the credit component from the equity option of convertible bonds. The main features of credit derivatives that make them particularly attractive for hedge funds are: they provide an efficient way to short a credit with a relatively low risk of a short squeeze, and they are better instruments for structuring any relative value trading strategies than bonds because they allow better alignment between maturities of different credit exposures. However, for "real money" accounts, CLNs represent a more viable investment alternative than CDSs, since these funds are typically allowed to invest only in cash instruments.[81] Since the ability of foreign investors to manage the emerging market corporate default risk remains limited (due to the relatively underdeveloped state of the corporate credit default markets), many emerging market borrowers are forced to issue bonds with various credit enhancements, particularly when the perceived credit risk is high (see Chapter V of IMF, 2002a).

The Role of Derivatives in Emerging Market Crises

While derivatives do play a positive role by reallocating risks and facilitating growth of capital flows to emerging markets, they can also allow market participants to take on excessive leverage, avoid prudential regulations, and manipulate accounting rules when financial supervision and internal risk management systems are weak or inadequate. In particular, the use (or rather misuse) of derivatives can potentially allow financial institutions to move certain exposures off balance sheets, thereby magnifying their balance sheet mismatches in ways that may not be easily

---

[79]See the notes on the index methodology on http://www.tremont.com.

[80]"Basis" is the difference between bond spread (over LIBOR) and the CDS premium for the same credit/same maturity.

[81]An important feature of CLNs is that they can be issued in Euroclearable form and listed on international exchanges. In contrast to CDSs, which do not pay the protection buyer until a credit event occurs, the credit-linked notes allow the protection buyer to receive cash payment at the time of the issuance of the notes, and thus eliminate the counterparty credit risk inherent in the CDSs. For more detailed discussion of various credit derivative products offered by major investment banks, see Deutsche Bank (2003) and Ranciere (2002).

CHAPTER IV THE ROLE OF FINANCIAL DERIVATIVES IN EMERGING MARKETS

detected by prudential supervisors and, as a result, may lead to a gradual buildup of financial system fragilities. Also, due to their very nature (i.e., the fact that they allow market participants to establish leveraged positions), derivative instruments tend to amplify volatility in asset markets. Thus, a negative shock to a country with already weak economic fundamentals, which typically triggers a sell-off in local asset markets, can also lead to an unpredictable and rapid unwinding of derivatives positions that can in turn accelerate capital outflows and deepen the crisis.

This section will discuss the role of derivatives in several emerging market crises focusing mainly on two issues: the types of financial derivatives used by market participants before the onset of a crisis and how the use of these instruments affected the stability of the domestic financial system; and the impact of the unwinding of derivatives positions on the crisis dynamics after the onset of a crisis. While the Mexican and Asian crises highlighted the role of structured notes and swaps in magnifying balance sheet mismatches and the associated volatility in foreign exchange markets, the Russian and Argentine crises demonstrated the importance of counterparty risk and spillovers through credit markets. It should be pointed out that deteriorating fundamentals—mostly fiscal, but also financial in the case of Asia—were the main causes of the recent emerging market crises, but derivatives amplified the impact of these crises on financial systems of emerging market economies. It should also be noted that the analysis of the role of derivatives in emerging market crisis is seriously hampered by data availability, since the OTC derivatives transactions are not reported systematically. Thus, in many cases, anecdotal evidence and reported (ex post) losses on derivatives positions by major investment banks of the industrial countries are the main sources of information.

The Mexican Crisis, 1994

In the early 1990s, the recently privatized Mexican banks engaged in an aggressive building up of their on- and off-balance sheet positions, which led to an increase of their credit and market risk exposures well beyond prudential limits. In particular, they used various derivatives to achieve leveraged returns. One of the popular instruments that allowed local banks to leverage their holdings of the exchange rate linked treasury bills (the Tesobonos) was a tesobono swap (Garber, 1998). In a tesobono swap, a Mexican bank received the tesobono yield and paid U.S. dollar LIBOR plus X basis points to an offshore counterparty, which in turn hedged its swap position by purchasing tesobonos in the spot market. The only transactions that were recorded in the balance of payments were: an outflow of bank deposits related to the payment of collateral by the Mexican bank, and a U.S. dollar inflow related to the purchase of tesobonos by the foreign investor. Thus, traditional balance of payments accounting provided a misguided representation of capital flows and associated risks—that is, although it appeared that the foreign investor had a long position in government bonds, it was in fact the local bank that bore the tesobono risk, while the foreign investor was effectively providing a short-term dollar loan. Tesobono swaps were not the only instruments that allowed local banks to establish leveraged positions financed by short-term U.S. dollar loans from their offshore counterparties; other instruments included various structured notes and equity swaps.[82]

At the onset of the crisis and in the face of rising political uncertainty and weakening fundamentals that ultimately forced the authorities to float the peso, the tesobono yields jumped from 8 percent to 24 percent. As a result, the U.S. dollar value of the collateral fell, triggering margin calls on Mexican banks.

---

[82]Equity swaps are a subset of the total return swaps that are discussed below.

Quoting market sources, Garber (1998) suggested that the total of margin calls on tesobono and total return swaps was about $4 billion, adding to the pressure on the Mexican peso foreign exchange market.[83]

The Asian Crises, 1997–98

As in the Mexican crisis, unhedged currency and interest rate exposures were key determinants of the severity and scope of the Asian crises (see IMF, 1998a). Banks and nonfinancial corporations in Asia left their exposures unhedged because (1) domestic interest rates were higher than foreign interest rates, (2) the pegged exchange rates were generally perceived as stable, and (3) domestic hedging products were underdeveloped, while offshore hedges were expensive. Because of these factors, foreign banks were eager to lend to East Asian banks that tried to capture carry profits on the interest rate differentials. However, local prudential regulations, such as restrictions on the net open foreign exchange exposures and risk-to-capital ratios, limited the amount of profitable arbitrage trade. Therefore, Asian financial institutions turned to derivatives "to avoid prudential regulations by taking their carry positions off balance sheet" (Dodd, 2001, p. 10).

According to market sources, the majority of losses reported by both U.S. and European banks on their Asian lending were listed as due to swap contracts, with the latter presumably including both total return swaps and currency swaps (Kregel, 1998). In a total return swap, one counterparty pays the other the cash flows (both capital appreciation and interest payments computed on a mark-to-market basis) generated by some underlying asset (equity, bond, or loan) in exchange for dollar LIBOR plus X basis points. Thus, the flows between Asian financial institutions and foreign counterparties were similar to those in the tesobono swap described above. As in the case of tesobono swaps, offshore counterparties were buying the underlying assets to hedge their swap positions, while local banks were left with short U.S. dollar positions. After weakening fundamentals led to a collapse of the exchange rate peg and domestic interest rates rose, both counterparties had incentives to either unwind the swaps or hedge their foreign exchange exposures, which exacerbated the sell-off in Asian assets and currencies.[84]

Russia's Default and Devaluation, 1998

Although the poor state of Russia's fiscal accounts was well known by mid-1998, the announcement of a 90-day moratorium on external debt payments on August 17, 1998 caught most market participants by surprise. At the time of the default and devaluation, the estimates of the outstanding notionals of the U.S. dollar-ruble NDF contracts ranged from $10 billion to $100 billion, and the total foreign exposure to the domestic bond market (GKO/OFZs) was around $20 billion. According to market sources, the U.S. dollar-ruble foreign exchange forwards with Russian firms as counterparties were the largest source of credit losses by major swap dealers during 1997–98, exceeding the losses made on their Asian lending. The events in Russia highlighted the presence of convertibility risk even when local currency positions in emerging markets were hedged, and raised the issue of the NDF valuation when an official rate was not available. In addition, Russia's default sent

---

[83]At the end of 1994, foreign exchange reserves of the Banco de Mexico were at $6.1 billion.

[84]Other structured instruments were also used in the run-up to the Asian crisis. For example, one of the well-known instruments was called a PERL—principal exchange rate linked note, described in detail in Dodd (2001). A PERL was a dollar-denominated instrument that generated cash flows linked to a long position in an emerging market currency. If the exchange rate remained stable, the return on the PERL was significantly higher than the return on the similarly rated dollar paper, but in the event of major depreciation, the return could become negative.

shock waves through the credit derivatives markets, with the cost of protection increasing in all sectors, including the investment-grade segment. Ambiguous and often misleading definitions of reference obligations, credit events, and settlement mechanics made it difficult for protection buyers to enforce the contracts. According to dealers, there was initially some confusion about which event had to trigger the credit default swap contracts—the declaration of the moratorium on debt payments or the actual default on obligations. In addition, it was unclear whether the CDS contracts that did not explicitly include cross-default clauses with the already restructured Soviet-era debt obligations (PRINs and IANs) had to be triggered by a default on these bonds. In order to address the legal issues highlighted during the Russian crisis, the International Swaps and Derivatives Association (ISDA) issued new credit derivative documentation guidelines in 1999.[85]

Argentina's Default and Devaluation, 2001

In contrast with the Russian crisis, the Argentine default and devaluation in December 2001 were widely anticipated and occurred at a time when the credit derivatives market was relatively more mature. The protracted recession and gradual deterioration of the sovereign's credit quality gave market participants sufficient time to exit the bond and credit protection markets and also allowed the main sellers of credit protection on Argentine sovereign bonds (broker-dealers) to hedge their books in the repo market. The liquidity in the Argentine CDS market dried up in August–September 2001, following a bout of volatility in July. The announcement of the moratorium on all debt payments on December 23, 2001 was unanimously accepted as a "repudiation/moratorium" credit event consistent with the ISDA definitions. There were, reportedly, some disputes as to which bonds could be considered as "deliverable," but they have been resolved fairly quickly. According to market sources, 95 percent of all credit default swaps were settled by mid-February 2002 and there were no reported failures to deliver, with the total notional amount of credit protection outstanding at the end of November 2001 estimated at $10–15 billion (see Deutsche Bank, 2003).[86]

Concluding Remarks

Local derivatives markets in emerging economies have grown rapidly over the past few years, especially in countries that have removed capital controls and have developed their underlying securities markets. The growing use of derivative products by emerging market participants has also supported capital inflows and has helped investors to price and manage the risks associated with investing in emerging markets more efficiently. However, the use of derivatives has also made crisis dynamics in some recent episodes more unpredictable by accelerating capital outflows, amplifying volatility, and, in some cases, increasing the correlation between asset and currency markets. In many of these episodes, the negative impact of derivatives on crisis dynamics was either due to the immaturity of local derivatives markets or due to weak prudential supervision, which allowed some financial institutions to build up leveraged positions before the onset of a crisis. The policy implications of the trends described in this chapter were discussed in a broader context of the development of local securities markets in Chapter I.

---

[85]The most recent (1999) ISDA guidelines include the following types of credit events: "failure to pay," "obligation acceleration," "obligation default," "repudiation/moratorium," and "restructuring."

[86]By comparison, as of November 2001, the value of the EMBI Global Argentina subindex was around $51 billion.

BIBLIOGRAPHY

Allen, Franklin, and Douglas Gale, 2000, *Comparing Financial Systems* (Cambridge, Mass.: MIT Press).

Bank for International Settlements, 2002a, *The Development of Bond Markets in Emerging Economies*, BIS Papers No. 11 (Basel: BIS).

———, 2002b, *Triennial Central Bank Survey: Foreign Exchange and Derivatives Market Activity in 2001*, March.

———, 2002c, *Quarterly Review*, June.

Barham, John, 2001, "A Compromise Solution," *Latin Finance* (October), pp. 40–43.

Beck, Thorsten, and Ross Levine, 2001, "Stock Markets, Banks and Growth: Correlation or Causality?" World Bank Policy Research Working Paper No. 2760 (Washington: World Bank, September).

Brooks, Robin, and Luis Catão, 2001, "The New Economy and Global Stock Returns," IMF Working Paper No. 00/216 (Washington: International Monetary Fund).

Bubula, Andrea, and Inci Ötker-Robe, 2002, "The Evolution of Exchange Rate Regimes Since 1990: Evidence from De Facto Policies," IMF Working Paper No. 02/155 (Washington: International Monetary Fund).

Burnside, Craig, Martin Eichenbaum, and Sergio Rebelo, 2001, "Hedging and Financial Fragility in Fixed Exchange Rate Regimes, *European Economic Review*, Vol. 45 (June), pp. 1151–93.

Caballero, Ricardo, 2002, "Coping with Chile's External Vulnerability: A Financial Problem," in *Economic Growth: Sources, Trends, and Cycles*, ed. by Norman Loayza and Raimundo Soto (Santiago, Chile: Central Bank of Chile).

———, and Arvind Krishnamurthy, 2003, "Excessive Dollar Debt: Financial Development and Underinsurance," *Journal of Finance*, Vol. 58 (April), pp. 867–93.

Calvo, Guillermo A., 1998, "Capital Flows and Capital Market Crises: The Simple Economics of Sudden Stops," *Journal of Applied Economics*, Vol. 1 (November), pp. 35–54.

———, 1999, "Contagion in Emerging Markets: When Wall Street Is the Carrier," Available on the Internet at http://www.bsos.umd.edu/econ/ciecalvo.htm.

———, 2000, "Capital Markets and the Exchange Rate: With Special Reference to the Dollarization Debate in Latin America," (unpublished; Center for International Economics, University of Maryland).

———, and Carmen M. Reinhart, 2000, "When Capital Inflows Suddenly Stop: Consequences and Policy Options," in *Reforming the International Monetary and Financial System*, ed. by Peter B. Kenen and Alexander K. Swoboda (Washington: International Monetary Fund).

Campbell, John Y., and Robert Shiller, 1996, "A Scorecard for Indexed Government Debt," in *NBER Macroeconomics Annual* (Cambridge: MIT Press).

Cervera, Alonso, and Audra Quedry, 2003, "Polling Mexico's Pension Funds," Credit Suisse First Boston (CSFB) Emerging Market Economics.

Cha, Hyeon-Jin, 2002, "Analysis of the Sluggish Development of the Secondary Market for Korean Government Bonds, and Some Proposals" (unpublished; Seoul: The Bank of Korea, Financial Markets Department, May).

Chan-Lau, Jorge, and Amadou Sy, forthcoming, "A Comparative Study of Sovereign Risk Measures, IMF Working Paper (Washington: International Monetary Fund).

Choe, Hyuk, Bong-Chan Kho, and René M. Stulz, 1999, "Do Foreign Investors Destabilize Stock Markets? The Korean Experience in 1997," *Journal of Financial Economics*, Vol. 54 (October), pp. 227–64.

Cifuentes, Rodrigo, Jorge Desormeaux, and Claudio Gonzalez, 2002, "Capital Markets in Chile: from Financial Repression to Financial Deepening," in BIS Papers No. 11, (Basel: BIS).

Claessens, Stijn, Simeon Djankov, and Larry H.P. Lang, 1998, "Who Controls East Asian Corporations?" World Bank Policy Research Working Paper No. 2054 (Washington: World Bank).

Claessens, Stijn, Daniela Klingebiel, and Sergio L. Schmukler, 2002, "Explaining the Migration of Stocks from Exchanges in Emerging Economies to International Centers," World Institute for

BIBLIOGRAPHY

Development Economic Research (WIDER) Discussion Paper No. WOP 2002/94. (Helsinki: United Nations University—WIDER).

Clement, Douglas, 2001, "The Vanishing Equity Premium," *The Region,* Federal Reserve Bank of Minneapolis (June).

Constantinides, George, John B. Donaldson, Rajnish Mehra, 2002, "Junior Can't Borrow: A New Perspective of the Equity Premium Puzzle," *Quarterly Journal of Economics,* Vol. 117, (February), pp. 269–96.

Credit Suisse First Boston/Tremont website: http://www.tremont.com.

Davies, Ben, 2002, "Equity Research—In Crisis?" *AsiaMoney* (November).

Deutsche Bank, 2000, "CE-3 Domestic Bond Markets," Global Markets Research.

———, 2001a, "Emerging Market Credit Derivatives," Global Markets Research.

———, 2001b, "The Malaysian Bond Market," Global Markets Research.

———, 2003, "Emerging Markets Credit Derivatives" (May).

Dodd, Randall, 2001, "The Role of Derivatives in the East Asian Financial Crisis," Economic Strategy Institute, The Derivatives Study Center, *http://www.econstrat.org.*

Dooley, Michael, 1996, "A Survey of the Literature on Controls over International Capital Transactions," *IMF Staff Papers,* International Monetary Fund, Vol. 43 (December), pp. 639–87.

———, 2000, "A Model of Crises in Emerging Markets," *The Economic Journal,* Vol. 110 (January), pp. 256–72.

Duffie, Darrell, 1999, "Credit Swap Valuation," *Financial Analyst Journal,* Vol. 55 (January/February), pp. 73–87.

Eichengreen, Barry, and Ricardo Hausmann, 1999, "Exchange Rates and Financial Fragility," NBER Working Paper No. 7418 (Cambridge, Mass.: National Bureau of Economic Research).

———, and Ugo Panizza, 2002, "Original Sin: The Pain, the Mystery, and the Road to Redemption" paper presented at the IDB Conference, "Currency and Maturity Matchmaking: Redeeming Debt from Original Sin (November).

Emerging Markets Investor, 2001, "Thinking Global, Buying Local," Vol. 8 (September), Issue 8.

Euroweek, 2001, "Converging Europe and Domestic Bond Markets" (September) Supplement.

Feldstein, Martin, 1999, "Self-Protection for Emerging Market Economies," NBER Working Paper No. 6907 (Cambridge, Mass.: National Bureau of Economic Research).

Fischer, Stanley, 2001, "Exchange Rate Regimes: Is the Bipolar View Correct?" *Journal of Economic Perspectives,* Vol. 15 (Spring), pp. 3–24.

Frankel, Jeffrey, and Sergio Schmukler, 1996, "Country Fund Discounts and the Mexican Crisis of 1994: Did Local Residents Turn Pessimistic Before International Investors?" *Open Economies Review,* Vol. 7 (Supplement 1), pp. 511–34.

Garber, Peter, 1998, "Derivatives in International Capital Flows," NBER Working Paper No. 6623, (Cambridge, Mass.: National Bureau of Economic Research).

Goldman Sachs, 2002, International Economic Analysis (April 2).

Greenspan, Alan, 1999, "Lessons from the Global Crises," remarks before the World Bank Group and the International Monetary Fund, Annual Meetings Program of Seminars, Washington, September 27. Available on the Internet at *http://www.federalreserve.gov/Boarddocs/Speeches/1999/199909272.htm.*

Hawkins, John, 2002, "Bond Markets and Banks in Emerging Economies," in *The Development of Bond Markets in Emerging Economies,* BIS Paper No. 11 (Basel: Bank for International Settlements).

Hayt, Gregory, and Richard Levich, 1999, "Who Uses Derivatives?" *Risk* (August).

Hong Kong Monetary Authority (HKMA), 2001, "Cost-Benefit Analysis of Developing Debt Markets," *Quarterly Bulletin* (November).

IFR, 2002, *Financing Begins at Home,* (June), pp. 65–66.

International Monetary Fund, 1995, *International Capital Markets: Developments, Prospects, and Key Policy Issues,* World Economic and Financial Surveys (Washington).

———, 1998a, *World Economic Outlook and International Capital Markets: An Interim Assessment,* World Economic and Financial Surveys (Washington).

———, 1998b, *International Capital Markets Developments: Prospects, and Key Policy Issues,* World Economic and Financial Surveys (Washington).

———, 1999, *International Capital Markets: Developments, Prospects, and Key Policy Issues,* World Economic and Financial Surveys (Washington).

_____, 2000, *International Capital Markets: Developments, Prospects, and Key Policy Issues,* World Economic and Financial Surveys (Washington).

_____, 2001, *International Capital Markets: Developments, Prospects, and Key Policy Issues,* World Economic and Financial Surveys (Washington, August).

_____, 2002a, *Global Financial Stability Report,* World Economic and Financial Surveys (Washington, March).

_____, 2002b, *Global Financial Stability Report,* World Economic and Financial Surveys (Washington, June).

_____, 2002c, *Global Financial Stability Report,* World Economic and Financial Surveys (Washington, September).

_____, 2002d, *Global Financial Stability Report,* World Economic and Financial Surveys (Washington, December).

_____, 2003a, "Exchange Arrangements and Foreign Exchange Markets Developments and Issues," World Economic and Financial Surveys (Washington: International Monetary Fund).

_____, 2003b, "Financial Stability in Dollarized Economies," (unpublished; Washington: Monetary and Exchange Affairs Department, International Monetary Fund).

_____, 2003c, *Global Financial Stability Report,* World Economic and Financial Surveys (Washington, September).

Jeanne, Olivier, 2002, "Why Do Emerging Economies Borrow in Foreign Currency?" paper presented at an IMF Research Department Seminar (Washington, March 6).

Johnson, Simon, and Andrei Shleifer, 2004, "Privatization and Corporate Governance," in *Governance, Regulation, and Privatization, in the Asia Pacific Region,* ed. by Takatoshi Ito and Anne O. Krueger (Chicago: University of Chicago Press).

Khor, Hoe E., 2001, "Derivatives and Macroeconomic Management in Post-Crisis Asia" (Monetary Authority of Singapore).

Kim, Woochan, and Shang-Jin Wei, 2002, "Foreign Portfolio Investors Before and During a Crises," *Journal of International Economics,* Vol. 56 (January), pp. 77–96.

Kregel, J.A, 1998, "Derivatives and Global Capital Flows: Applications to Asia," *Cambridge Journal of Economics,* Vol. 22, pp. 677–692.

La Porta, Rafael, Florencio Lopez-de-Silanes, Andrei Shleifer, and Robert Vishny, 2000, "Investor Protection and Corporate Governance," *Journal of Financial Economics,* Vol. 58 (Issues 1–2), pp. 3–27.

Merrill Lynch, 2001, "Size and Structure of the World Bond Market: 2001," Global Fixed Income Strategy.

_____, 2002, "Size and Structure of the World Bond Market: 2002," Global Fixed Income Strategy.

Montagu-Pollock, Matthew, 2001, "Gagged, Pressured and Compromised," *Asiamoney,* (October), pp. 17–21.

Moody's Investors Services, 2001, "Asia's Domestic Capital Markets: Works in Progress," Special Comments, Global Credit Research.

_____, 2002, "Malaysia's Debt Capital Markets Assume New Importance," Special Comments, Global Credit Research.

Norton, Guy, 2002, "The Fall and Rise of Rouble Bonds," *Euroweek* (October).

Organization for Economic Cooperation and Development, 2001, "Bond Market Development in Asia" (Paris: OECD).

Pagano, Marco, Otto Randl, Alisa Röell, and Josef Zechner, 2001, "What Makes Stock Exchanges Succeed? Evidence from Cross-Listing Decisions," CEPR Discussion Paper No. 2683 (London: Centre for Economic Policy Research).

Parsons, Nick, 2001, "The Bond Markets in Asia," *Euroweek* (June).

Patel, Navroz, 2002, "The Vanilla Explosion," *Risk* (February).

Prasad, Eswar, Kenneth Rogoff, Shang-Jin Wei, and Ayn Kose, 2003, *Effects of Financial Globalization on Developing Countries: Some Empirical Evidence,* Occasional Paper No. 220 (Washington: International Monetary Fund).

Ranciere, Romain, 2002, "Credit Derivatives in Emerging Markets" (unpublished; New York: New York University, Stern School of Business).

Ransley, Anuszka, 2002, "Eastern Europe: Game On," *FOW* (May).

Reinhart, Carmen M., and Kenneth S. Rogoff, 2002, "The Modern History of Exchange Rate Arrangements: A Reinterpretation," NBER Working Paper No. 8963 (Cambridge, Massachusetts: National Bureau of Economic Research).

BIBLIOGRAPHY

Roldos, Jorge, 2003, "Pension Reform and Capital Markets" (unpublished; Washington: International Monetary Fund).

Salomon Smith Barney, 2002, "Equity Strategy" (March 5).

Schinasi, Garry, and R. Todd Smith, 1998, "Fixed Income Markets in the United States, Europe, and Japan: Some Lessons for Emerging Markets," IMF Working Paper No. 173/98 (Washington: International Monetary Fund).

_____, R. Sean Craig, Burkhard Drees, and Charles Kramer, 2000, *Modern Banking and OTC Derivatives Markets: The Transformation of Global Finance and Its Implications for Systemic Risk*, IMF Occasional Paper No. 203 (Washington: International Monetary Fund).

Sharma, Krishnan, 2000, "The Underlying Constraints on Corporate Bond Market Development in South East Asia," United Nations, DESA Discussion Paper No. 14 (September).

Shy, Oz, and Juha Tarkka, 2001, "Stock Exchanges, Access Fees, and Competition," Bank of Finland Discussion Paper No. 22.

Steil, Benn, 2001, "Borderless Trading and Developing Securities Markets," in *Open Doors: Foreign Participation in Financial Systems in Developing Countries*, ed. by Robert E. Litan, Paul Masson, and Michael Pomerleano (Washington: Brookings Institution Press).

Walker, Eduardo, 2002, "The Chilean Experience with Completing Markets with Financial Indexation," in *Inflation and Monetary Policy*, ed. by Le-Fort and Schmidt-Hebbel (Santiago: Central Bank of Chile).

World Bank, and IMF, 2001, *Developing Government Bond Markets: A Handbook* (Washington: World Bank).

Yam, Joseph, 2001, "Developing and Positioning Hong Kong's Bond Market," speech delivered at the Forum on China's Government Securities Market in the New Century (Hong Kong, November 19). Available on the Internet at *http://www.info.gov.hk/hkma/eng/speeches/index.htm*.

Yuan, Kathy, 2000, "Information Externality of Sovereign Bonds on the Liquidity of Corporate Bonds: An Empirical Exploration," (unpublished; Cambridge: Massachusetts Institute of Technology, April).

World Economic and Financial Surveys

This series (ISSN 0258-7440) contains biannual, annual, and periodic studies covering monetary and financial issues of importance to the global economy. The core elements of the series are the World Economic Outlook report, usually published in May and October, and the semiannual Global Financial Stability Report. Other studies assess international trade policy, private market and official financing for developing countries, exchange and payments systems, export credit policies, and issues discussed in the World Economic Outlook. Please consult the IMF Publications Catalog for a complete listing of currently available World Economic and Financial Surveys.

World Economic Outlook: A Survey by the Staff of the International Monetary Fund

The World Economic Outlook, published twice a year in English, French, Spanish, and Arabic, presents IMF staff economists' analyses of global economic developments during the near and medium term. Chapters give an overview of the world economy; consider issues affecting industrial countries, developing countries, and economies in transition to the market; and address topics of pressing current interest.

ISSN 0256-6877.
$49.00 (academic rate: $46.00); paper.
2003. (April). ISBN 1-58906-212-4. **Stock #WEO EA 0012003.**
2002. (Sep.). ISBN 1-58906-179-9. **Stock #WEO EA 0022002.**
2002. (April). ISBN 1-58906-107-1. **Stock #WEO EA 0012002.**

Exchange Arrangements and Foreign Exchange Markets: Developments and Issues
by a staff team led by Shogo Ishii

This study updates developments in exchange arrangements during 1998–2001. It also discusses the evolution of exchange rate regimes based on de facto policies since 1990, reviews foreign exchange market organization and regulations in a number of countries, and examines factors affecting exchange rate volatility.

ISSN 0258-7440
$42.00 (academic rate $35.00)
2003 (March) ISBN 1-58906-177-2. **Stock #WEO EA 0192003.**

Official Financing: Recent Developments and Selected Issues
by a staff team in the Policy Development and Review Department led by Martin G. Gilman and Jian-Ye Wang

This study provides information on official financing for developing countries, with the focus on low-income countries. It updates the 2001 edition and reviews developments in direct financing by official and multilateral sources.

$42.00 (academic rate: $35.00); paper.
2003. ISBN 1-58906-228-0. **Stock #WEO EA 0132003.**
2001. ISBN 1-58906-038-5. **Stock #WEO EA 0132001.**

Exchange Rate Arrangements and Currency Convertibility: Developments and Issues
by a staff team led by R. Barry Johnston

A principal force driving the growth in international trade and investment has been the liberalization of financial transactions, including the liberalization of trade and exchange controls. This study reviews the developments and issues in the exchange arrangements and currency convertibility of IMF members.

$20.00 (academic rate: $12.00); paper.
1999. ISBN 1-55775-795-X. **Stock #WEO EA 0191999.**

World Economic Outlook Supporting Studies
by the IMF's Research Department

These studies, supporting analyses and scenarios of the World Economic Outlook, provide a detailed examination of theory and evidence on major issues currently affecting the global economy.

$25.00 (academic rate: $20.00); paper.
2000. ISBN 1-55775-893-X. **Stock #WEO EA 0032000.**

Global Financial Stability Report: Market Developments and Issues

The Global Financial Stability Report, published twice a year, examines trends and issues that influence world financial markets. It replaces two IMF publications—the annual International Capital Markets report and the electronic quarterly Emerging Market Financing report. The report is designed to deepen understanding of international capital flows and explores developments that could pose a risk to international financial market stability.

$49.00 (academic rate: $46.00); paper.
September 2003 ISBN 1-58906-236-1. **Stock #GFSR EA0022003.**
March 2003 ISBN 1-58906-210-8. **Stock #GFSR EA0012003.**
December 2002 ISBN-1-58906-192-6. **Stock #GFSR EA0042002.**
September 2002 ISBN 1-58906-157-8. **Stock #GFSR EA0032002.**
June 2002 ISBN 1-58906-131-4. **Stock #GFSR EA0022002.**

International Capital Markets: Developments, Prospects, and Key Policy Issues (back issues)
$42.00 (academic rate: $35.00); paper.
2001. ISBN 1-58906-056-3. **Stock #WEO EA 0062001.**

Toward a Framework for Financial Stability
by a staff team led by David Folkerts-Landau and Carl-Johan Lindgren

This study outlines the broad principles and characteristics of stable and sound financial systems, to facilitate IMF surveillance over banking sector issues of macroeconomic significance and to contribute to the general international effort to reduce the likelihood and diminish the intensity of future financial sector crises.

$25.00 (academic rate: $20.00); paper.
1998. ISBN 1-55775-706-2. **Stock #WEO-016.**

Trade Liberalization in IMF-Supported Programs
by a staff team led by Robert Sharer

This study assesses trade liberalization in programs supported by the IMF by reviewing multiyear arrangements in the 1990s and six detailed case studies. It also discusses the main economic factors affecting trade policy targets.

$25.00 (academic rate: $20.00); paper.
1998. ISBN 1-55775-707-0. **Stock #WEO-1897.**

Available by series subscription or single title (including back issues); academic rate available only to full-time university faculty and students. For earlier editions please inquire about prices.

The IMF Catalog of Publications is available on-line at the Internet address listed below.

Please send orders and inquiries to:
International Monetary Fund, Publication Services, 700 19th Street, N.W.
Washington, D.C. 20431, U.S.A.
Tel.: (202) 623-7430   Telefax: (202) 623-7201
E-mail: publications@imf.org
Internet: http://www.imf.org